REVISE EDEXCEL
FUNCTIONAL SKILLS ENTRY LE...

Mathematics

REVISION GUIDE

Series Consultant: Harry Smith

Author: Sharon Bolger

To revise all the topics covered in this book, check out:

Revise Functional Skills Entry Level 3
Mathematics Workbook   978 1 292 145600

Also in this series:

Revise Functional Skills Level 1
Mathematics Revision Guide   978 1 292 145693

Revise Functional Skills Level 2
Mathematics Revision Guide   978 1 292 145709

THE REVISE SERIES
For the full range of Pearson revision titles, visit:
www.pearsonschools.co.uk/revise

Contents

A small bit of small print

Edexcel publishes Sample Test Materials on its website. This is the official content and this book should be used in conjunction with it. The questions in *Now try this* have been written to help you practise every topic in the book. Remember: the real test questions may not look like this.

Whole numbers

It is important to know the size of numbers used in everyday life.

Using numbers

You will use numbers to:

✓ count objects or money

✓ measure lengths and weights of objects

✓ order quantities

✓ label items.

245 is a three-digit number.

Digits

A number is made up of digits.

There are 10 digits that we use to make numbers: 0, 1, 2, 3, 4, 5, 6, 7, 8 and 9

2 4 5

2, 4 and 5 are all digits

The position of each digit tells you its value and helps you to read the number.

The more digits a whole number has, the larger the number.

Worked example

1 (a) Write the number 32 in words.

Thirty-two

  (b) Write the number 345 in words.

Three hundred and forty-five

  (c) Write the number two hundred and forty-seven in figures.

247

  (d) Write the number four hundred and six in figures.

406

	hundreds	tens	units
(a)		3	2
(b)	3	4	5
(c)	2	4	7
(d)	4	0	6

This 3 means 3 tens.

This 3 means 3 hundreds.

This 0 means no tens.

Worked example

2 Write down the value of the digit 3 in:

  (a) 2306   3 hundreds or 300

  (b) 230   3 tens or 30

  (c) 403   3 units or 3

The zeros in these numbers show the place value of the other digits.

Without the zero in the number 403, the number would be 43, which has a different value.

Now try this

1 How many digits are there in the whole number 63?

2 (a) Write the number 521 in words.

  (b) Write the number 602 in words.

  (c) Write the number four hundred and two in figures.

  (d) Write the number five hundred and twenty in figures.

3 Write down the value of the 4 in each of these numbers.

  (a) 432   (b) 341   (c) 234

Comparing numbers

You can compare whole numbers by looking at the number of digits.

The fewer the digits in a whole number, the smaller the number. So 45 is smaller than 452 as it has fewer digits.

When two numbers have the same number of digits, you need to look at the place value of each digit.

4 5
↑ ↑
two digits

4 5 2
↑ ↑ ↑
three digits

Value of digits

The numbers 234 and 432 contain the same digits but have different values.

432 is larger than 234

You can see which number is larger by looking at the value of the first digit, reading from the left.

If both numbers have the same first digit, look at the value of the second digit.

587 is larger than 549

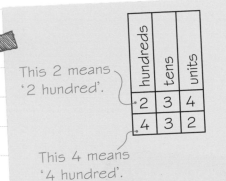

This 2 means '2 hundred'.

hundreds	tens	units
2	3	4
4	3	2

This 4 means '4 hundred'.

Worked example

1 (a) Which number is larger, 496 or 469? 496
  (b) Which number is smaller, 202 or 220? 202
2 Order these amounts from smallest to largest.
  £506   £803   £223   £83

£83   £223   £506   £803

83 is the smallest number as it has the fewest digits.

Start from the largest place value. The digits are the same.

The digits are the same.

hundreds	tens	units
4	9	6
4	6	9
2	0	2
2	2	0

9 tens is larger than 6 tens. 496 is larger than 469

The digits are different so compare. 202 is smaller than 220

Now try this

1 Which of these numbers is the largest?
  204, 302, 320
2 Using the digits 4, 9 and 2:
  (a) make the largest number possible   (b) make the smallest number possible.
3 An engineering company has parts listed as numbers in its database.
  Order these part numbers from smallest to largest.
  234, 243, 203, 230

Adding

In some questions you will need to add numbers.

The symbol for addition is **+**

Using addition

In the test, you may not be told which calculation to do, so you need to decide.

Sometimes it will involve adding numbers together.

You can use your calculator to work out the answer.

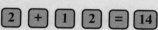

Worked example

1. A waiter has two customers.

   The first customer leaves £2 in tips.
   The second customer leaves £12 in tips.

   How much did the waiter earn in tips altogether?

   2 + 12 = £14

Remember to include the units in your answer. In this example, the units are in pounds (£).

Worked example

2. Martin records the number of hours he worked in five months.

Month	Number of hours
January	98
February	116
March	141
April	110
May	120

   How many hours did Martin work in total?

   98 + 116 + 141 + 110 + 120 = 585
   Martin worked 585 hours.

 To work out how many hours Martin worked in total, you need to add the number of hours worked each month. You can use a calculator to help.

 There are five months in the table, so check that you have added up five numbers.

 Don't forget to put the units in your answer.

Now try this

1. Manfred sells a bicycle for £349 and a helmet for £94.
   How much does Manfred make in total?

2. The table shows the number of clients a window cleaning business had each week in February. What was the total number of clients in February?

	Clients
Week 1	146
Week 2	52
Week 3	129
Week 4	114

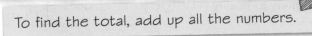

To find the total, add up all the numbers.

Subtracting

In some questions you will need to subtract numbers.

The symbol for subtraction is ―

Worked example

1 Maria pays for a box of biscuits with a
   £5 note. The biscuits cost £3.
   How much change does she get?

   5 − 3 = 2
   She gets £2 change.

You can use your calculator to work out the answer.

Remember to include the units in your answer.

Worked example

2 Paul has a piece of fabric that is 432 cm long.
   He cuts the fabric to make a cushion cover.
   He needs one piece of fabric that is 150 cm long
   and another piece that is 35 cm long.
   How long is the remaining piece of fabric?

   432 − 150 − 35 = 247
   The remaining piece of fabric is 247 cm.

Another way to work out the answer to this calculation is:
✓ find the total length of fabric he cuts
150 + 35 = 185 cm
✓ then subtract this amount from 432
432 − 185 = 247 cm

Worked example

3 Samira buys and sells watches.
   She buys the watches for £235 each and sells
   them for £548 each. How much profit does she
   make on each watch?

   £548 − £235 = £313

profit = amount earned − cost to buy

Now try this

1 Jason spends 8 hours at work every day. He is either in the office or making deliveries.
   On one day, Jason spends 3 hours making deliveries. How many hours does he spend in the office?
2 Fernando buys and sells second hand mobile phones. He buys each phone for £35 and sells them for
   £72. How much profit does Fernando make on each phone?
3 Claire has a £10 note. She spends £4 on lunch. She wants to buy
   a notebook, which costs £8. Does she have enough money to buy
   the notebook?
4 The table shows the amount of money earned by a charity shop on
   four days in a week.
   The total amount earned for Monday to Friday is £950. How much does
   the charity shop earn on Friday?

Day	Amount raised
Monday	£120
Tuesday	£220
Wednesday	£235
Thursday	£194

Multiplication

In some questions you will need to use multiplication.

The symbol for multiplying numbers is ✕

Worked example

1 There are 25 chocolate bars in a box.
A shop buys 3 boxes of chocolate bars.
How many chocolate bars does the shop buy?

$25 \times 3 = 75$ chocolate bars

> Multiplication is repeated addition.
> 3×25 is the same as $25 + 25 + 25$

> You can do this calculation on your calculator.
>

Worked example

2 Carl works each week from Monday to Friday.
He travels to and from work by bus and spends £8 each day on his bus tickets.
How much does it cost him to travel to and from work each week?

$5 \times 8 = 40$

It costs him £40 to travel to work.

Problem solved!

Read the question carefully.
Monday to Friday means 5 working days:
Monday, Tuesday, Wednesday, Thursday, Friday

Carl spends £8 each day to travel so the calculation will be multiplication.

Don't forget to put the units in your answer.

Multiply the number of hours Mavis studies per day by the number of days.

For more about working with time, look at page 29.

Worked example

3 Tereza studies from 9.00 a.m. to 12.00 noon each day.
How many hours does she study for in 10 days?

From 9.00 a.m. to 12.00 noon is 3 hours.

$3 \times 10 = 30$ hours

Now try this

1 Work out 23×8

2 A coach can hold 52 people. How many people can 5 coaches hold?

3 Kevin wants to buy 12 cartons of juice. Each carton costs £2. Kevin has £25, does he have enough money?

4 The cost of parking a car in a car park for the whole day is £7.
Sharon parks her car in the car park for the whole day on 5 days a week for 4 weeks. How much does it cost her to park her car?

5 Emina buys tickets to the cinema for herself and 3 friends.
A ticket costs £17. How much does Emina spend on tickets?

> Be careful – how many tickets does Emina need to buy?

Division

In some questions you will need to use division.

Division is the same as 'sharing'. The symbol for division is $\div$

Worked example

1 Fatima makes 20 cakes. She packs them in boxes that hold 5 cakes each. How many boxes does she need?

$20 \div 5 = 4$ boxes

You can use a calculator.

This is a question about sharing items out equally so you need to use division.

If 20 cakes are shared out equally in boxes that hold 5 cakes each, then there are 4 boxes of cakes.

Worked example

2 Emil and 3 friends have dinner in a restaurant.

The bill comes to £92.

They decide to split the bill equally.

How much is each person's share?

There are 4 people including Emil.

$92 \div 4 = 23$

Each person pays £23.

Don't forget to write your answer in pounds (£).

Worked example

3 Clare makes a picture frame from a piece of wood that measures 90 cm.

She cuts the wood into 6 pieces of the same length. How long is each piece of wood?

$90 \div 6 = 15$ cm

Remember to write the units in your answer.

Worked example

4 Freddie gets paid £380 per week. He works a 38 hour week.

How much does he get paid per hour?

$380 \div 38 = £10$ per hour

Problem solved!

Read the question carefully to decide what calculation you need to do.

The question asks about how much he gets paid per hour so you need to divide.

Now try this

1 Work out $300 \div 12$

2 Antoni is an event organiser. He buys tickets to a concert for a group of 14 friends. He spends £252 in total. How much was each ticket?

3 252 chairs will be set up in 7 rows. How many chairs need to be in each row?

Multiplying and dividing by 10, 100 and 1000

It is useful to know how to multiply and divide by 10, 100 and 1000 when you work with money and with units of length, weight and capacity.

For more about units see page 33

Multiplying by 10, 100, 1000

	thousands	hundreds	tens	units
				7
× 10			7	0
× 100		7	0	0
× 1000	7	0	0	0

Fill the empty spaces with zeros.

When multiplying by 10, each digit moves one place to the left.

When multiplying by 100, each digit moves two places to the left.

When multiplying by 1000, each digit moves three places to the left.

Worked example

A magnifying glass makes items appear 10 times as big as they really are. An insect is 9 mm long. How long does it look in the magnifying glass?

$9 \times 10 = 90$ mm

10 times bigger than 9 mm means 10×9 mm

Dividing by 10 and 100

	hundreds	tens	units		tenths	hundredths
	2	4	0			
÷ 10		2	4			
÷ 100			2	.	4	

When dividing by 10, each digit moves one place to the right.

When dividing by 100, each digit moves two places to the right.

Now try this

1. Work out: **(a)** 12×10 **(b)** 3×100 **(c)** $520 \div 10$
2. Work out: **(a)** 1×1000 **(b)** 1.2×100 **(c)** $1000 \div 100$

Remainders

If you can't divide one amount exactly by another, the amount left over is called a remainder. Mia shared 7 mints between her friends, Julie and Mark.

Using a calculator,
$7 \div 2 = 3.5$

If the answer is a decimal, there is a remainder. Each person cannot have 0.5 of a mint so they will get 3 mints each.

7 mints shared between 2 people
$7 \div 2$

Julie   Mark

Julie and Mark get 3 mints each and there is 1 left over. The remainder is 1

1 A teacher had 18 coloured pencils that she shared equally between 5 students.
   How many pencils did each student get?

$18 \div 5 = 3.6$

You can't have 0.6 of a pencil, so each student got 3 pencils and 3 were left over.

You can do this question on your calculator.

In this question, you will need to **round down** to the nearest whole number.

Worked example

2 Diego is organising a party.
   He needs to buy 42 cartons of juice.
   The cartons come in packs of 10.
   (a) How many packs should Diego buy?

$42 \div 10 = 4.2$

Diego needs to buy 5 packs of cartons.

   (b) How many drinks will he have left over?

$5 \times 10 = 50$
$50 - 42 = 8$

Diego will have 8 cartons left over.

✓ Read and understand the question.
✓ Decide which calculation to perform.
✓ Decide whether to round up or down to the next whole number.

Diego cannot buy 4.2 packs of drink and 4 packs is not enough, so **round up**. Diego needs to buy 5 packs to have enough.

If Diego buys 5 packs of drink, and there are 10 drinks in each pack, he will buy 50 drinks altogether.

Now try this

1 Moira has 156 roses.
   She needs 10 roses to fill a vase of flowers.
   (a) How many vases can she fill?
   (b) How many roses are left over?

2 Zan is organising a trip for 140 people.
   A coach can hold 56 people.
   How many coaches does he need to hire?

Choosing the right order

Sometimes you will need to do more than one calculation to answer a question.

You will need to be able to choose the correct order for the calculations.

Worked example

1 Hasan is paid £2,000 per month after tax. His bills are:

Rent	£630
Electricity and gas	£82
Council tax	£75
Telephone	£42
Water	£26

How much does he have left when he pays his bills?

630 + 82 + 75 + 42 + 26 = £855

2000 − 855 = 1145

Hasan has £1,145 left.

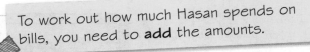

To work out how much Hasan spends on bills, you need to **add** the amounts.

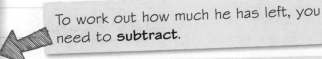

To work out how much he has left, you need to **subtract**.

Check your answer is sensible. It should be less than Hasan earns.

Worked example

2 A shop buys 36 USB sticks for a total of £252 and sells them for £13 each.

Work out how much profit the shop makes.

£13 × 36 = £468

£468 − £252 = £216

Don't forget to write your answer in pounds (£).

Problem solved!

Read the question carefully. You need to show all your working out so it is clear how you approached the problem.

✔ Work out how much the shop sold all the sticks for in total. To do this, calculate price per stick × number of sticks

✔ To find the profit, subtract the amount the shop paid for the sticks from the total amount they sold the sticks for.

Now try this

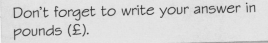

1 Lewis earns £520 per week. He spends £80 on rent and £60 on bills each week.

How much does he have left?

2 Part of the menu at a cafe is shown on the right.

Mavis orders a coffee, a sandwich and a muffin.

She pays with a £10 note. How much change does she get?

3 Ben makes jewellery. A bracelet costs him £3 to make and he sells it for £8.

Ben sells 10 bracelets. How much profit does he make?

cafe	
coffee	£2
tea	£1
sandwich	£3
ice cream	£2
muffin	£3

Using a calculator

You can use a calculator in the test, so you need to know how to use it properly.

It's important to check your answer when you use a calculator as it is easy to press the wrong buttons.

The display shows you the buttons you have pressed and your anwer.

This clears the calculator so you can start a new calculation.

Press this to insert a decimal point.

See page 22 for more on checking your answer.

These are the buttons you will press to do your calculations.

Press the equals button to get your answer.

✓ Always make sure the display shows 0 before you start.

✓ Make sure you press the correct buttons on your calculator.

✓ Remember to press the = sign to get your answer.

Worked example

1 Carlos wants to buy a new TV.

In one shop the TV costs £350. The same TV in another shop is £420.

What is the difference in price?

420 − 350 = 70

The difference in price is £70

4 2 0 − 3 5 0 = 70

Be careful when interpreting the answer from a calculator. 70 means £70.

Worked example

2 A piece of plastic is 200 cm long.

Oscar cuts the plastic into 4 equal pieces.

How long is each piece of plastic?

200 ÷ 4 = 50

Each piece of plastic is 50 cm.

2 0 0 ÷ 4 = 50

Remember to write the units in your answer. 50 in this calculation means 50 cm.

Now try this

1 A concert ticket costs £52. How much will 4 tickets cost?

2 A conference table can seat 4 people. If 112 people attend a conference, how many tables are needed?

Multiples

You need to be able to recognise and use multiples. You need to practise and learn the multiplication facts to help you recognise multiples.

Multiples

The multiples of a number are all the numbers in its times table.

The multiples of 5 are 5, 10, 15, 20, 25…

You can look at the last digit of a number to find out whether it is a multiple of 2, 5, 10, 50 and 100.

✓ Multiples of 2 end with 0, 2, 4, 6 or 8

✓ Multiples of 5 end with 0 or 5

✓ Multiples of 10 end with 0

✓ Multiples of 50 end with 50 or 100

✓ Multiples of 100 end with 00

> Even numbers are multiples of 2. Numbers that are not multiples of 2 are called odd numbers.

Worked example

1 Look at the number square.

1	2	3	4	5
6	7	8	9	10
11	12	13	14	15
16	17	18	19	20
21	22	23	24	25

(a) Which of the numbers in the square are multiples of 5?

5, 10, 15, 20, 25

(b) List the even numbers in the square.

2, 4, 6, 8, 10, 12, 14, 16, 18, 20, 22, 24

Worked example

2 Bhavik uses five 50p coins to buy a bus ticket worth £2.50. Does he get any change?

No, because five 50p coins are worth exactly £2.50 so Bhavik will not get any change.

> £2.50 = 250p, which is a multiple of 50. So it must be possible to pay for a £2.50 ticket exactly with 50p coins.

3 Aashi wants to stay on the third floor of a hotel. The available rooms on the third floor are 354, 367, 309 and 300.

In this hotel, even numbered rooms are ensuite. Which available rooms on the third floor are ensuite?

354 and 300

> Look for numbers in the list that end in 0, 2, 4, 6 or 8.

Now try this

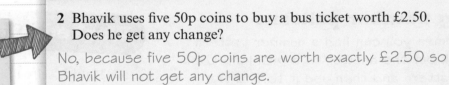

> Write down the first five numbers in the 3 times table and the first five numbers in the 4 times table.

1 Write the first five multiples of:
   (a) 3   (b) 4

2 Tara works in a hiking shop. The shop stocks boots from size 3 to size 12. Even sizes go on the top shelf and odd sizes go on the bottom shelf. Which sizes of boots are on the bottom shelf?

3 Bill uses a £1 coin and two 50p coins to buy a chocolate bar for £2.00. Will he receive any change?

Number patterns

A number pattern is a list of numbers that follow a pattern. You can use number patterns to solve problems.

Spotting number patterns

A number pattern might be a list of numbers that always increase or decrease by a certain amount.

3, 7, 11, 15, 19, ... increases by 4
+4 +4 +4 +4

20, 17, 14, 11, 8, ... decreases by 3
−3 −3 −3 −3

Other number patterns are lists of numbers that are always multiplied or divided by the same amount.

1, 3, 9, 27, 81, ... multiplied by 3
×3 ×3 ×3 ×3

32, 16, 8, 4, 2, ... divided by 2
÷2 ÷2 ÷2 ÷2

You can describe a number pattern by saying what happens to each number in the list to get to the next number.

Worked example

1 Ava opens a business that sells mobile phones. The table show how many mobile phones Ava sells in the first five months of trading.

Jan	Feb	Mar	Apr	May
5	10	20	40	80

Describe what happens to the number of phones she sells each month.

The number of phones Ava sells doubles each month.

Each number in the list is equal to the previous number multiplied by two. 'Double' means 'multiply by 2' so you can say the number of phones doubles each month.

Using number patterns

Sometimes you can find a number pattern to work out the answer to a problem. Look for a pattern and then use it to find the next number in the list.

Look for a number pattern. Matilda sells 5 T-shirts each day so subtract 5 from each number to get the next number.

Worked example

2 Matilda sells T-shirts at a market. She sells the same number of T-shirts each day.

She starts with 80 T-shirts.
After one day, she has 75.
After two days, she has 70.
After three days, she has 65.

How many T-shirts does she have left after 4 days?

80 → 75 → 70 → 65 → 60
She has 60 T-shirts left after 4 days.

Now try this

Jeremy sells carpets. On Monday he sells 5 carpets. Each day that week, his target is to sell 3 more carpets than he did the previous day.

How many carpets does he need to sell on Wednesday to meet his target?

Decimals

Decimals are numbers in between whole numbers. They are written with a decimal point.

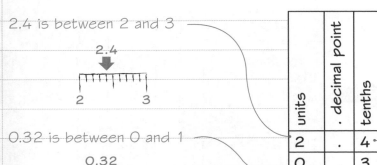

2.4 is between 2 and 3

0.32 is between 0 and 1

units	. decimal point	tenths	hundredths
2	.	4	
0	.	3	2

You would say this number as 'two point four'.

You would say this number as 'zero point three two'.

Digits on the right of the decimal point have a value less than 1

Worked example

1 Which two whole numbers do these numbers lie between?

  (a) 43.7   43 and 44

  (b) 2.1   2 and 3

  (c) 3.05   3 and 4

You can use a number line to help.

43.7

43   44

43.7 is closer to 44 than to 43

Worked example

2 Write down the value of the digit 7 in:

  (a) 3.79   7 tenths

  (b) 98.07   7 hundredths

  (c) 7.03   7 units

In the number 98.07, the '0' is important to show the place value of the 7. Without the zero the number would be 98.7 which has a different value.

Decimal places

The number 12.3 has one digit after the decimal point. This number has one decimal place.

The number 3.42 has two digits after the decimal point. This number has two decimal places.

Now try this

1 Write whole numbers to complete the sentences.

  (a) 6.5 is between............... and...............   **(b)** 0.36 is between............... and...............

2 Write down the value of the digit 3 in: **(a)** 4.35   **(b)** 2.03

3 Complete this sentence.   14.3 is a number with .... decimal place.

Ordering decimals

You will sometimes need to compare decimals and put them in order.

Worked example

1 (a) Which number is larger, 0.04 or 0.4?

0.4

(b) Which number is larger, 1.02 or 1.03?

1.03

Start from the largest place value. The units are the same.

The units and the tenths are the same.

	units	. decimal point	tenths	hundredths
(a)	0	.	0	4
	0	.	4	
(b)	1	.	0	2
	1	.	0	3

4 tenths is larger than 0 tenths so 0.4 is larger than 0.04

3 hundredths is larger than 2 hundredths so 1.03 is larger than 1.02

Zeros in decimal numbers

3.6 is the same as 3.60

hundreds	tens	units	. decimal point	tenths	hundredths
		3	.	6	
		3	.	6	0

3.6 and 3.60 are the same. They both have 0 hundredths.

Numbers with one decimal place can be written to two decimal places by adding a '0'.

The '0' doesn't change the value if there aren't any digits after it.

Worked example

2 A carpenter has some lengths of wood. Order the lengths from smallest to largest.
0.3 m, 0.03 m, 0.02 m, 0.32 m

0.02, 0.03, 0.3, 0.32

Write the numbers to two decimal places to help you compare them. 0.3 is the same as 0.30

Now try this

Look at the highest place value in both numbers first. If the digits are the same, look at the next place value.

1 Write the largest number in each of these pairs of numbers.
   (a) 6.72 and 6.27
   (b) 23.8 and 23.08
2 The amounts paid for materials by a builder are listed below. Order the amounts from smallest to largest.
   £22.30   £22.03   £23.02   £20.30

Fractions

A fraction is part of a whole. A fraction is made of equal parts.
Here is the flag of France.

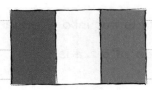

one part is blue → **1** ← numerator
out of → ———
3 equal parts → **3** ← denominator

Common fractions

You need to know these common fractions and be able to recognise them written in words.

This shape has 2 equal parts so one part is $\frac{1}{2}$

This shape has 5 equal parts so one part is $\frac{1}{5}$

a half $\frac{1}{2}$ a third $\frac{1}{3}$ a quarter $\frac{1}{4}$ a fifth $\frac{1}{5}$ a tenth $\frac{1}{10}$

Worked example

1 What fraction of this shape is shaded?

$\frac{1}{5}$ is shaded.

2 Which of these shapes is split into quarters?

shape B

> The diagram is divided into 5 equal parts so the denominator is 5
> 1 part is shaded so the numerator is 1

> Shape B has been split into 4 equal parts so each part is a quarter.

Golden rule

Fractions of a shape must be equal.
4 unequal parts are not the same as quarters.

The number of equal parts is the denominator of the fraction.

Now try this

1 What fraction of this shape is shaded grey?

> The denominator is the number of equal parts.

2 Write these fractions in words.   **(a)** $\frac{1}{4}$ **(b)** $\frac{1}{3}$ **(c)** $\frac{1}{10}$

Types of fractions

The denominator (bottom number) of a fraction tells you how many parts something has been divided into. The numerator (top number) of a fraction tells you how many of the parts you're talking about.

Fractions are divisions

The fraction line is like a ÷ sign. The diagram shows 1 whole pizza divided into 6 parts, so each part is worth 1 ÷ 6.

$\frac{1}{6}$ is another way of writing 1 ÷ 6.

A pizza is cut into 6 equal pieces.

1 piece of pizza is $\frac{1}{6}$

2 pieces is $\frac{2}{6}$

The whole pizza = $\frac{6}{6}$ or 1

Each of the yellow parts is $\frac{1}{4}$ and there are 3 yellow parts.

$\frac{1}{4} + \frac{1}{4} + \frac{1}{4} = \frac{3}{4}$

You can say $\frac{3}{4}$ as 'three-quarters'.

Worked example

1 (a) What fraction of this shape is pink?

$\frac{1}{4}$

(b) What fraction of this shape is yellow?

$\frac{3}{4}$

Worked example

2 Amal bought 3 bags of flour. He used 1 of them to make scones.

What fraction of the quantity of flour he bought does he have left?

3 − 1 = 2 so he has 2 bags of flour left.

He has 2 bags left out of 3, so the fraction he has left is $\frac{2}{3}$

First work out how many bags Amal has left. Then work out what this number is as a fraction of the total number of bags.

You can say $\frac{2}{3}$ as 'two-thirds'.

Now try this

1 What fraction of this shape is

(a) shaded black? $\frac{2}{5}$

(b) shaded green? $\frac{1}{5}$

(c) not shaded? $\frac{2}{5}$

2 Write $\frac{4}{5}$ as a fraction in words. Four Fifths

Equivalent fractions

Some fractions have the same value but look different. These are called equivalent fractions.

Calculating equivalents

$\frac{1}{2}$ of a pizza is the same amount as $\frac{2}{4}$ of a pizza.

$\frac{1}{2}$ and $\frac{2}{4}$ are equivalent fractions.

You can work out whether fractions are equivalent by dividing.

$\frac{1}{2}$ means $1 \div 2$ and $\frac{2}{4}$ means $2 \div 4$ so use your calculator to work out these calculations.

$1 \div 2 = 0.5$

$2 \div 4 = 0.5$

The calculations have the same answer so the fractions are equivalent.

If the numerator and the denominator are the same, the fraction is equal to 1.

$$\frac{1}{1} = \frac{2}{2} = \frac{3}{3} = \frac{10}{10} = \frac{100}{100} = 1$$

Fraction wall

A fraction wall is a good way of seeing equivalent fractions.

1							
$\frac{1}{2}$				$\frac{1}{2}$			
$\frac{1}{4}$		$\frac{1}{4}$		$\frac{1}{4}$		$\frac{1}{4}$	
$\frac{1}{8}$	$\frac{1}{8}$	$\frac{1}{8}$	$\frac{1}{8}$	$\frac{1}{8}$	$\frac{1}{8}$	$\frac{1}{8}$	$\frac{1}{8}$

Worked example

A garage has some oil left in 1-litre tins. The fraction of oil in each tin is:

$\frac{1}{4}$ $\frac{2}{8}$

If the fractions are equivalent, the tins contain the same amount of oil.

Do the tins contain the same amount of oil?

$1 \div 4 = 0.25$

$2 \div 8 = 0.25$

$\frac{1}{4}$ and $\frac{2}{8}$ are equivalent so there is the same amount of oil in the tins.

$\frac{1}{4}$ means $1 \div 4$ and $\frac{2}{8}$ means $2 \div 8$

Use your calculator to work out whether the division calculations have the same answer.

Now try this

1 (a) Is $\frac{3}{4}$ equivalent to $\frac{6}{8}$? *Yes*

   (b) Is $\frac{1}{5}$ equivalent to $\frac{2}{8}$? *NO*

   (c) Is $\frac{3}{8}$ equivalent to $\frac{6}{16}$? *Yes*

2 Which of these fractions is equivalent to $\frac{1}{3}$?   *$\frac{2}{6}$* $\frac{3}{6}$ $\frac{4}{6}$

3 Which of these fractions is equivalent to 1? $\frac{2}{4}$ *$\frac{7}{7}$* $\frac{6}{3}$

Fractions of amounts

You need to be able to find fractions of amounts so that you can solve problems.

Unit fractions of amounts

You can find a fraction of an amount by dividing. If the numerator of the fraction is 1, divide the amount by the denominator.

To find $\frac{1}{4}$ of £24,

divide £24 into 4 equal parts.

£24 ÷ 4 = £6

Worked example

1 Work out
   (a) $\frac{1}{4}$ of £80

£80 ÷ 4 = £20

   (b) $\frac{1}{2}$ of 60 g

60 g ÷ 2 = 30 g

2 Sixteen people are divided into four teams of equal size. How many people are in each team?

16 ÷ 4 = 4 people

If there are 4 teams of equal size, each team has $\frac{1}{4}$ of the total number of people.

Worked example

3 Ali wants to buy a silver necklace. He sees this advertisement.

Sterling silver
charm necklace
$\frac{1}{2}$ of normal price
normal price = £160

How much will this necklace cost?

$\frac{1}{2}$ of £160

£160 ÷ 2 = £80

The denominator of the fraction is 2, so divide £160 by 2. Remember to write your answer in pounds.

Now try this

Use your answer to part (a) to help you work out part (b).

Work out: **(a)** $\frac{1}{2}$ of £60   **(b)** $\frac{1}{4}$ of £60   **(c)** $\frac{1}{4}$ of 48 g

£30   £15   12g

Rounding whole numbers

It can be useful to round a number when you don't need to know or use its exact value. Numbers that are rounded are easier to understand and easier to use in rough calculations.

Rounding to the nearest 10

To round to the nearest 10, look at the multiples of 10 that the number lies between.

32 lies between 30 and 40

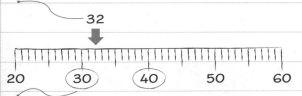

32 is closer to 30 so 32 is rounded down to 30

If the digit in the units column is 5 or more, round up. If the number in the units column is less than 5, round down.

32 is less than 35, so round down.

Rounding to the nearest 100

When rounding to the nearest 100, look at the multiples of 100 that the number lies between.

670 lies between 600 and 700

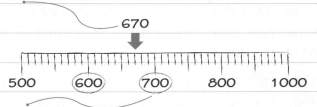

670 is closer to 700 so 670 is rounded up to 700

If the digit in the tens column is 5 or more, round up. If the number in the units column is less than 5, round down.

670 is more than 650, so round up.

Worked example

1 (a) A piece of plastic measures 26 cm. Round this to the nearest 10.

26 cm rounded to the nearest 10 is 30 cm.

(b) The width of a table top is 155 cm. Round this number to the nearest 10.

155 cm rounded to the nearest 10 is 160 cm.

2 A college prospectus reports how many students are members of the college, rounded to the nearest 100. This year, there are 211 students in the college. What is the number stated in the prospectus?

211 rounded to the nearest 100 is 200.

When rounding to the nearest 10, look at the closest multiples of 10. You could sketch a number line to help.

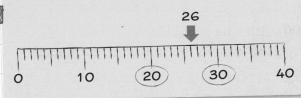

155 is exactly halfway between 150 and 160, so round up.

You need to round to the nearest 100, so look at the number in the tens column. 211 is less than 250, so round down.

Now try this

1 Round these numbers to the nearest 10.
   (a) 65   70   (b) 323   320
2 Round these numbers to the nearest 100.
   (a) 435   400   (b) 571   600
3 Alfie earned £827 last week. Round this number to the nearest 100.   800

Rounding money

When calculating with money, you will work in either pounds and pence or only pence.
The symbol for pounds is £, and the symbol for pence is p.

£1.26   126p

1 pound 26 pence   126 pence

Rounding to the nearest pound

To round money to the nearest pound, look at the first digit after the decimal point.

If the first digit after the decimal point is 5 or more, round up.

£2.65 to the nearest pound is £3

> When you round **up** to the nearest pound, add 1 to the number of pounds.

If the first digit after the decimal point is less than 5, round down.

£2.45 to the nearest pound is £2

> When you round **down** to the nearest pound, the number of pounds stays the same.

Worked example

(a) Oliver paid £8.56 for his shopping.
Round this to the nearest pound.

£8.56 is £9 to the nearest pound.

> £9 is the same as £9.00 because the number of pence is 0

(b) Alejandro paid £128.30 for a table.
How much is this to the nearest pound?

£128.30 is £128 to the nearest pound.

> Make sure your answer is a whole number of pounds.

(c) A packet of lentils costs £1.15
What is the price of the packet of lentils to the nearest pound?

£1

Now try this

1 Round these amounts to the nearest pound.
   (a) £6.70 £7   (b) £8.38 £8
   (c) £256.55 £257   (d) £420.50 £421
2 Tamar bought stationery costing £3.82. How much was this to the nearest pound? £4
3 Potatoes cost £1.50 per kg. How much is this to the nearest pound? £2
4 Peter pays £435.50 each month on rent. How much is this to the nearest pound? 436
5 Julie paid £5.36 for her lunch one day. She said this is £6 to the nearest pound. Is Julie correct? Give a reason for your answer. NO. 5.36 IS closer to £5

Estimating

Estimating the answer to a calculation is useful when you don't need to know the exact answer. Estimating will give you an answer that is a little bit more or a little bit less than the exact answer. You can estimate by rounding numbers.

There is more about rounding on page 19.

Estimating with rounding

You can estimate the answer to a calculation by rounding the numbers to the nearest 10 or 100

✓ If the number is between 10 and 99, round to the nearest 10

✓ If the number is between 100 and 999, round to the nearest 100

Use this symbol when rounding and estimating:

$$\approx$$

$429 \approx 400$ means 429 is approximately equal to 400

Worked example

1 (a) Work out an estimate for 58 + 31

58 and 31 rounded to the nearest 10 are:
$58 \approx 60$
$31 \approx 30$
$58 + 31 \approx 60 + 30 \approx 90$

(b) Work out an estimate for 429 − 287

429 and 287 rounded to the nearest 100 are:
$429 \approx 400$
$287 \approx 300$
$429 - 287 \approx 400 - 300 \approx 100$

Use the $\approx$ sign to show that your answers are not exact.

Worked example

2 Fernando claimed his travel expenses for three train journeys.
He spent £6.54, £2.31 and £9.50.
Estimate how much he spent on travel.

$£6.54 \approx £7$
$£2.31 \approx £2$
$£9.50 \approx £10$
$£7 + £2 + £10 = £19$

Round each amount to the nearest £1 then add them together.

Your answer is an estimate of how much Fernando spent. £19 is close to how much he actually spent.

Now try this

1 Estimate the answer to:

(a) 58 + 71 130

(b) 892 − 312 600   900 − 300

(c) 48 × 9 500   50 × 90

2 Sarah went shopping for some new stationery. She bought a pen for £2.99 and a notepad for £5.20. Estimate how much she spent.   3 + 5 = 8

Checking your answer

It is easy to press the wrong button on your calculator and make a mistake. You should always check your answer is correct.

Using estimation to check your answer

You can use estimation after doing a calculation to check if your answer is sensible.

> Look at page 21 for how to estimate the answer to a calculation.

> The question asks you to check whether the answer is correct, so write a statement saying whether it is correct as part of your answer.

Worked example

1 Portia said the answer to
59 + 32 − 42 is 174
Check whether she is correct.

$59 \approx 60$
$32 \approx 30$
$42 \approx 40$
$60 + 30 - 40 = 50$

This is a lot lower than 174 so she has made a mistake in her calculation.

Using inverse operations

You can check your answer is correct by using inverse or opposite operations.

- Adding and subtracting are inverse operations.
- Multiplying and dividing are inverse operations.

Worked example

2 Samuel said the answer to 40 − 22 is 18.
Check whether he is correct using inverse operations.

$40 - 22 = 18$
$18 + 22 = 40$
Samuel is correct.

> You should always get the number you started with.

Worked example

3 Sheila worked out 12 × 5 and got the answer 70.
Check whether she is correct.

If $12 \times 5 = 70$
then $70 \div 5$ must equal 12
$70 \div 5 = 14$
Sheila is not correct.

> You could also check by working out
> $70 \div 12$ and seeing if the answer is 5.
> You will have a calculator in the test so you can use it to check your answer.

Now try this

1 Carl worked out the answer to this calculation:
82 + 98 − 89 = 1895
Show that he is incorrect by estimating the answer to the calculation.

$80 + 100 = 180$
$180 - 90 = 90$

2 Use inverse operations to check if these are correct.
   (a) 423 + 239 = 662   (b) 39 + 323 = 335   (c) 53 × 31 = 1590   (d) 872 ÷ 2 = 436

Problem-solving practice

When you are solving problems, you need to:

- ✓ read the question
- ✓ check your answers
- ✓ decide which calculation you are going to use
- ✓ make sure you have answered the question asked.

 Here is part of the menu at a cafe.

cafe	
large coffee	£3
small coffee	£2
large tea	£2
small tea	£1
slice of cake	£3

Josie orders 2 small coffees and a slice of cake.

How much change does she get from a £10 note?

Choosing the right order page 9

Read the question carefully.

Work out how much Josie spends on 2 small coffees and a slice of cake.

Subtract this from £10 to see how much change she gets.

TOP TIP

Work out the cost of 2 small coffees first – then add the cost of a slice of cake. This will give you the total cost.

 Saskia owns a bicycle shop.

One week, she buys 80 bicycles to sell in her shop.

She sells $\frac{1}{4}$ of the bicycles for £300 each.

(a) How much money does Saskia receive for the bicycles? 6,000

(b) Saskia buys another bicycle for £437.
She sells it for £923.
How much profit does she make?

Fractions of amounts page 18 and Subtracting page 4

Work out how many bicycles Saskia sells.

Then work out how much Saskia makes when she sells each of these bicycles for £300.

TOP TIP

The profit is the difference between how much money Saskia makes and how much she spends. You can work it out by subtracting.

 Martin is making up packets of screws for flat packed tables. He has 188 screws.

Each packet needs 10 screws.

(a) How many packets of screws can he make? 18

(b) How many screws are left over? 8

Remainders page 8

Work out how many 10s are in 188.

It will not be an exact number so there will be a remainder.

The remainder will be the number of screws that are left over.

TOP TIP

Set out your working to clearly show your calculations.

23

Had a go ☐   Nearly there ☐   Nailed it! ☐

Problem-solving practice

 4 Elizabeth is booking a seat on a train. The available seats are numbered 14, 27, 90, 134, 145 and 149.

Elizabeth wants a window seat in the quiet carriage. Window seats have even numbers. Seats in the quiet carriage have numbers between 100 and 150. Which of these seats should Elizabeth choose?

134

Multiples page 11

Write down the even numbers in the list. Then find which of the even numbers is between 100 and 150.

TOP TIP

Remember to answer the whole question. If a number is even but is not between 100 and 150, it is not the correct answer.

---

 5 Shona has a business selling T-shirts. Each week, she wants to sell 4 more T-shirts than she did the previous week.

In week 1 she sells 10 T-shirts.

(a) Complete the table to show how many T-shirts she wants to sell each week.

week 1	week 2	week 3	week 4	week 5
10	14	18	22	26

(b) How many T-shirts does she want to sell in week 6? 30

Number patterns page 12

Add 4 to each number to find the next one.

TOP TIP

Check your working by using inverse operations.

---

 6 Here is a receipt from Yusef's shopping.

Receipt

£2.39   2
£8.87   9
£4.26   4
£0.99   1
£2.28   2
        18

Work out an estimate for the cost of Yusef's shopping.

Estimating page 21

Round each amount to the nearest whole number.

Add these numbers to work out an estimate.

TOP TIP

Make sure you write down the rounded numbers before adding them.

---

 7 Martin is training for a 100m athletics race. Here are five of his times.

12.40 seconds 2
12.04 seconds 1
12.47 seconds 3

Order the times from shortest to longest.

Ordering decimals page 14

The tens and the units are the same in all three numbers so look at the digits after the decimal point.

TOP TIP

Read the question carefully.

Remember to start with the smallest number.

Calendars

You need to be able to use a calendar and work out the number of days between given dates.

A calendar shows you the dates and days of the week in a month.

This calendar shows the dates in February 2016.

	February 2016					
Mo	**Tu**	**We**	**Th**	**Fr**	**Sa**	**Su**
1	2	3	4	5	6	7
8	9	10	11	12	13	14
15	16	17	18	19	20	21
22	23	24	(25)	26	27	28
29						

The days of the week are the top row.

The numbers show the dates.

There are 7 days in one week.

25 February is a Thursday.

You can write dates in different formats. You could write 25 February 2016 as 25/02/2016 or 25/2/16.

Worked example

This calendar shows the month of July.

	July					
Mo	**Tu**	**We**	**Th**	**Fr**	**Sa**	**Su**
	1	2	3	4	5	
6	7	8	9	10	11	12
13	14	15	16	(17)	18	19
20	21	22	23	24	25	26
27	28	29	30	31		

(a) Simon goes on holiday for 5 nights. He leaves on the third Friday in July. What day does he return?

Wednesday 22 July

(b) Simon needs to go shopping for his holiday on the Saturday before he leaves. On what date does he need to go shopping?

Saturday 11 July

To find the date when Simon leaves for his holiday:
- ✔ Look in the Friday column of the calendar.
- ✔ Find the third Friday in July.
- ✔ Circle this date – 17 July.
- ✔ Count the 5 nights he will be away. Include the day he leaves as this will be his first night away.

- ✔ Look in the Saturday column of the calendar.
- ✔ Find the Saturday before Simon leaves for his holiday, which is on the row above.

Now try this

Look at the calendar above showing July.

(a) What date is the second Saturday of the month? 11th

(b) Mark books a hotel from 9 July for 10 nights. What date does he leave the hotel? 19th

(c) A customer at a garage books his car in on 7 July. He is told the car will be ready on the Thursday of the following week. What is the date of Thursday in the following week?

16th

25

Units of time

You need to be able to use time measured in years, days, hours, minutes and seconds.

Time facts

1 minute = 60 seconds

1 hour = 60 minutes

1 day = 24 hours

1 week = 7 days

1 year = 365 days

You can talk about time using fractions of an hour.

15 minutes = a quarter of an hour

30 minutes = half an hour

45 minutes = three quarters of an hour

> 1 hour = 1 × 60 mins
> 2 hours = 2 × 60 mins

Worked example

1 How many minutes are in 2 hours?

1 hour = 60 minutes

So 2 hours will be:

2 × 60 = 120 minutes

2 Alan is preparing a meal. He needs a quarter of an hour to chop ingredients and half an hour to cook them. How long does he need in total? Write your answer in minutes.

$\frac{1}{4}$ hour = 15 minutes

$\frac{1}{2}$ hour = 30 minutes

15 + 30 = 45 minutes

> $\frac{1}{2}$ of 60 minutes means
> 60 minutes ÷ 2 = 30 minutes

Worked example

2 The table shows the amount of time Sam spent on certain types of exercise.

Task	Time
running	2 hours
football	60 minutes
cross training	15 minutes
yoga	3 hours

What was the total time Sam spent exercising?

Football: 60 minutes = 1 hour

Cross training: 15 minutes = $\frac{1}{4}$ hour

$2 + 1 + \frac{1}{4} + 3 = 6\frac{1}{4}$ hours

> Convert the times in minutes into hours. Then add the times together to get your answer.

> 15 minutes is the same as $\frac{1}{4}$ of an hour or 'a quarter of an hour'.

Now try this

James spends $4\frac{1}{2}$ hours working and 30 minutes travelling to work. What is the total time James spends travelling and working?   5

12-hour clock

You need to be able to read and write times using the 12-hour clock.
This is an analogue clock. In the 12-hour clock, it shows 2 o'clock.

The large hand of the clock points to the minutes.

Each small division around the clock face represents 1 minute.

The small hand of the clock points to the hours.

Fractions of an hour

In 1 hour there are 60 minutes.

15 minutes is $\frac{1}{4}$ hour.

30 minutes is $\frac{1}{2}$ hour.

45 minutes is $\frac{3}{4}$ hour.

Morning or afternoon

When you write a time using the 12-hour clock, you need to say whether the time is:

- in the morning – a.m.
- in the afternoon or evening – p.m.

Telling the time

You can tell the time using the 12-hour clock in words or in figures. These clocks all show times in the morning.

This clock shows half past 4 in the morning, or 4.30 a.m.

This clock shows quarter past 1 in the morning, or 1.15 a.m.

This clock shows quarter to 4 in the morning, or 3.45 a.m.

Worked example

This clock tells the time in a train station one evening.
Write this time using the 12-hour clock.

8.30 p.m. or half past 8 in the evening.

Remember to write a.m. or p.m. to show whether it is morning or afternoon.

Now try this

These clocks show times after midday. Write the times they show in words and numbers.

(a)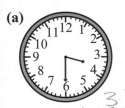

(b)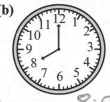

(c)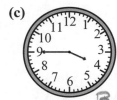

3.30
Half Past 3

8.00
EIGHT o'clock

3.45
quarter to 4

27

24-hour clock

This clock tells the time in a train station one afternoon.

In the 12-hour clock this would be written as 2.45 p.m.

In the 24-hour clock this would be written as 14:45

Converting between the 12-hour clock and the 24-hour clock

In the 12-hour clock you have to write whether it is a.m. (morning) or p.m. (afternoon).

12-hour clock	24-hour clock
1.15 a.m.	01:15
3.40 p.m.	15:40
12.00 midday	12:00
12.00 midnight	00:00

In the 24-hour clock, if the first two digits are less than 12, it is morning.

If the first two digits are 12 or more, it is afternoon.

For times in the morning, the hours and the minutes are the same in the 12-hour clock and the 24-hour clock.

1.15 a.m. (12-hour) is the same as 01:15 (24-hour).

For times in the afternoon or evening, add 12 hours to convert from the 12-hour clock to the 24-hour clock. Take away 12 hours to convert from the 24-hour clock to the 12-hour clock.

4.50 p.m. ──[+12]──▶ 16:50
12-hour clock ◀──[−12]── 24-hour clock

Worked example

1 (a) Andrea left home at 8.20 a.m. to go to work.
Write this time using the 24-hour clock.

08:20

(b) She left work at 5.45 p.m.
Write this time using the 24-hour clock.

17:45

Add 12 onto the hours as the time is in the afternoon.

Worked example

2 Will finished work at 19:26.
Write this time using the 12-hour clock.

7.26 p.m.

Take away 12 from the hours in the 24-hour clock.

╭─ 19:26 ─╮
The hours change.　　The minutes
19 − 12 = 7　　stay the same.

Now try this

1 This clock shows the time in the afternoon.

2.45

(a) Write this time using the 12-hour clock.
(b) Write this time using the 24-hour clock. 14:45

2 Complete this table of times in the 12-hour and 24-hour clock.

12-hour	24-hour
3.12 a.m.	03:12
7:50 pm	19:50
11.30 p.m.	21:30
2:15 pm	14:15

Time calculations

You can use time calculations to solve real-life problems, like deciding when you need to set off to catch a train.

> Look at page 27 and page 28 for a reminder of how to write time.

Worked example

1 Harris has a lesson that starts at 2.00 p.m.
The lesson lasts for 50 minutes.
Write down the time that the lesson finishes.

2.50 p.m.

Add 50 minutes onto the minutes to work out the time.

hours   minutes

2.00 p.m. afternoon
+ 50 minutes
2.50 p.m.

2 Rav makes some bread dough at 11:45 in the morning. It needs to be left in a warm place for 3 hours before he puts it in the oven.

What time should the he put it in the oven? Write your answer using the 24-hour clock.

14:45

hours   minutes

11:45
+ 3 hours
14:45

Worked example

3 Manuel needs to catch the 11:00 train.

(a) It takes him 15 minutes to walk to the station.
What is the latest time he can leave home to catch his train?

10:45

(b) The journey takes 1 hour and 30 minutes.
What time does Manuel arrive at his destination?

12:30

It is useful to draw a timeline to add and subtract minutes and hours.

−15 minutes

10:00   10:45   11:00

+1 hour   +30 minutes

11:00   12:00   12:30

Now try this

1 Joshua catches a bus at 13:45. 14:00
The journey takes 15 minutes.
What time does Joshua reach his destination?

2 Noam works from 09:00 until 12:00. How many hours does he work? 3hrs

3 Sarah is visiting family in Manchester. She leaves home at 08:00 and drives for 3 hours and 30 minutes.
What time does she arrive in Manchester? 11.30am

Timetables

Reading timetables is a skill that you will use when travelling. You will need to learn how to read timetables and work out how long journeys will take.

This table shows part of a bus timetable.

Timetables usually give times using the 24-hour clock.

Great Malvern	07:15	08:15	09:45	11:15
Barnard's Green	07:30	08:30	10:00	11:30
Guarlford Road	07:45	08:45	10:15	11:45

This bus leaves Barnard's Green at 11:30 and arrives at Guarlford Road at 11:45, so the journey takes 15 minutes.

This bus leaves Great Malvern at 09:45 and arrives at Guarlford Road at 10:15.

Worked example

This table shows part of a train timetable from Richgate to Riflesbury.

Richgate	11:10	11:30	11:50
Palace Gardens	11:20	11:40	12:00
Riflesbury	11:25	11:45	12:05

(a) Joseph catches the 11:30 train from Richgate. What time does he arrive at Palace Gardens?

11:40

Find the 11:30 train in the row for Richgate. Look down the column to find the time it arrives at Palace Gardens.

(b) Zuzanna got on the train at Richgate and arrived in Riflesbury at 11:25. What time train did she catch at Richgate?

11:10

Find the train that arrives in Riflesbury at 11:25 and work out what time it leaves Richgate.

(c) How long was Zuzanna's journey?

Zuzanna set off at 11:10 and arrived at 11:25.
25 − 10 = 15 so the journey took 15 minutes.

Find the arrival time and the departure time, then work out how far apart they are in minutes.

Now try this

The timetable shows the train times from King's Park to Dyston.

King's Park	05:45	06:00	06:15	06:30	06:45
Dyston	05:55	06:10	06:25	06:40	06:55

(a) Ying got on the 06:15 train at King's Park. What time did she arrive in Dyston?  06·25

(b) (i) Simon needs to get to Dyston before 06:50. Which is the latest train he can catch from King's Park?
   (ii) How long does the journey take? 06·30

Problem-solving practice

When you are solving problems, you need to:

- ✓ read the question
- ✓ check your answers
- ✓ decide which calculation you are going to use
- ✓ make sure you have answered the question asked.

---

1 The calendar shows the days in May.

	May 2016						
Mo	Tu	We	Th	Fr	Sa	Su
						1
2	3	4	5	⑥	7	8
9	10	11	12	13	14	15
16	17	18	19	20	21	22
23	24	25	26	27	㉘	29
30	31					

Joe needs a birthday cake by 28 May.

Today is Friday 6 May.

The baker needs 10 working days to make the cake and can start today.

The baker does not work at weekends.

Will the cake be ready on time? *Yes*

Calendars page 25

Put your finger on 6 May.

Count 10 working days. Remember working days are Monday to Friday inclusive.

TOP TIP

Make sure you answer the question that has been asked – you must write a statement to say whether Joe will get his cake in time for the birthday.

---

2 The table shows the amount of time a teacher spends on different tasks one morning.

Task	Time
teaching a class	2 hours
planning the next lesson	30 minutes
marking homework	45 minutes
paperwork	15 minutes

How long does the teacher work that morning?
Give your answer in hours and minutes. *3hrs 30mins*

Units of time page 26

Add up the number of minutes.
Convert this to hours and minutes and then you can add the number of hours.

TOP TIP

Remember, 60 minutes is 1 hour.

---

3 Jennifer is on a hiking trip. She starts walking at 08:30.

She walks for 2 hours and then has a break for 30 minutes. *11*

She walks for a further 2 hours and then has lunch for 1 hour.

She then walks for another 3 hours before reaching the campsite.

What time does she reach the campsite?
Write your answer using the 24-hour clock. *17.00*

Time calculations page 29

Draw a table to help.

starts walking	08:30
start of break	10·30
walking	11·00
start of lunch	13·00
walking	14 – 17
reaches campsite	17·00

TOP TIP

As your answer is needed in the 24-hour clock, write the times in the table in the 24-hour clock.

31

Problem-solving practice

 Here is part of a bus timetable.

North St	09:50	10:20	10:50
Mill Hill Rd	10:15	10:45	11:15
Pottergate	10:30	11:00	11:30

Akiko arrives at North St at 09:45.
She wants to catch the earliest bus to Pottergate.

(a) At what time does her bus leave North St? 09:50

(b) What time does she arrive in Pottergate? 10:30

(c) How long does the journey take? 40mins

Timetables page 30

Find the next time after 09:45 that a bus leaves North St.

Look at the same column in the timetable to find out when the train arrives at Pottergate.

TOP TIP

Write the length of the journey in minutes.

5 The clocks show the time that Mark starts and finishes a test in the afternoon.

starts the test   finishes the test

12-hour clock page 27, 24-hour clock page 28, Time calculations page 29

In the 24-hour clock, the first two digits are bigger than 12 for times in the afternoon.

TOP TIP

You can use the clock face to help you work out how long the test is.

(a) What time does Mark start the test? 1:30   13:30
Write the time using the 24-hour clock.

(b) What time does Mark finish the test? Write 17:00
the time using the 24-hour clock.

(c) How long is the test?   3 ½ hrs

Units

You need to know how to use measurements for length, capacity, weight and temperature. There are two measuring systems called metric and imperial.

Length

You measure a distance to see how long it is.

Kilometres and metres are metric units of length.

Miles are an imperial unit of length.

Temperature

You measure a temperature to see how hot it is.

You will usually measure temperature in degrees Celsius (°C) but you may also see it in degrees Fahrenheit (°F).

Capacity

You measure a capacity to see how much a container can hold.

Litres and centilitres are metric units of capacity.

Pints are an imperial unit of capacity.

Weight

You measure a weight to see how heavy it is.

Tonnes and kilograms are metric units of weight.

Pounds and stones are imperial units of weight.

Worked example

Which of these measuring instruments would you use to measure a quantity of milk?

A   B   C

C measuring jug

The measuring jug is most suitable because you can't measure the length of milk and you don't usually need to know the weight of milk.

Now try this

1 Choose the most suitable units from the list to complete the sentences:
   metres, degrees Celsius, pint, kilograms

   (a) A shop sells 2 _Pint_ bottles of milk. The milk is stored in a fridge at 5_°C_ .

   (b) Bob is buying a new kitchen. The width of the kitchen is 4.5 _metres_. His kitchen table is flat-packed and weighs 25 _kilograms_

2 Frank measured the weight of an egg and said it was about 20 cm. Is he correct? Explain your reasons.
   No, cm are used to measure length not weight

Length

Lengths can be measured using different units.

Units of length

Metric units of length are kilometres (km), metres (m) and centimetres (cm).

Feet and inches are imperial units of length.

You can convert between metric units of length by multiplying by 10, 100 or 1000.

For a reminder of multiplying by 10, 100 and 1000 look at page 7.

Metric lengths
1 km = 1000 m
1 m = 100 cm
1 cm = 10 mm

To change kilometres to metres, multiply by 1000.

To change metres into centimetres, multiply by 100.

To change centimetres into millimetres, multiply by 10.

Make sure lengths are in the same units before you do any calculations.

Worked example

1 Write the metric unit you would use to measure each of the following.

   (a) The distance between two towns

   kilometres

   (b) The length of a pencil

   centimetres

Sometimes there is more than one unit that might be a sensible choice. You might use centimetres or millimetres to measure the length of a pencil.

Worked example

2 Tamar cycled 6 miles to the park. She then cycled another 3.5 miles.

   How far did she cycle altogether?

   6 + 3.5 = 9.5 miles

3 Inaki has a piece of fencing that is 3 m long. He buys another piece of fencing that is 120 cm long.

   What is the total length of fencing he has now?

   3 m = 3 × 100 = 300 cm
   300 cm + 120 cm = 420 cm

Before you can add, the lengths must be in the same units.

1 m = 100 cm so 3 m = 3 × 100 cm

Now try this

1 Choose the largest quantity in each list.
   (a) 5 m   520 cm   ④ 4 km
   (b) ① 1 foot   1 inch

2 Noel joins two pieces of nylon. One piece is 3 feet long, the other piece is 2.5 feet long. What is the total length of the nylon?   5·5 feet

3 Mary has a piece of rope which is 6 m long. She cuts it into three equal sections. How long is each section of rope?   2m

4 A plant is 5 cm tall. In one week it grows by 3 mm. How tall is the plant at the end of the week?

   5·3 cm   53 mm

Measuring lengths

You need to be able to use a ruler to draw and measure straight lines accurately. Don't measure lines in your exam unless the question tells you that the diagram is accurate or 'to scale'.

Worked example

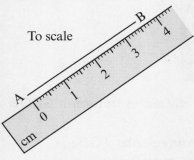

To scale

Measure the length of the line AB.

3.5 cm

Line up the 0 mark on your ruler carefully with the start of the line at A.

Always measure to the nearest mm on a ruler.

Make sure your ruler doesn't move while you're measuring the line.

Don't forget to write the units with your answer.

This line is 35 mm or 3.5 cm long.

There is more about cm and mm on page 34.

Drawing lines checklist

- ✓ Check whether you are working in cm or mm.
- ✓ Start the line at the 0 mark on your ruler.
- ✓ Hold your ruler firmly.
- ✓ Use a sharp pencil.
- ✓ Draw to the nearest mm.
- ✓ Label the length you have drawn.

Estimating

You can use lengths that you know to estimate other lengths.

The child is 1 m tall.

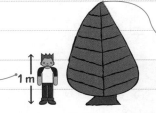

1 m

You can see that the tree is about twice as tall as the child. A good estimate for the height of the tree is 2 × 1 m = 2 m

Now try this

Measure to the nearest millimetre.

1   Measure the lengths of these lines.

   (a) _____   **(b)** _____

2   The picture of a bus and a dolphin have been drawn accurately to the same scale. The real length of the dolphin is 3 m. Estimate the real length of the bus.

Reading scales

You need to be able to read scales and number lines. Scales are used to measure quantities.

Reading a scale

To read a scale, begin by working out what each division on the scale represents.

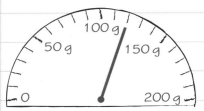

There are five divisions between 100 g and 150 g.

Each division represents 10 g.

The scale reads 120 g.

Not all divisions represent one unit or ten units.

There are two divisions between 600 g and 800 g.

Each division represents 100 g.

The scale reads 700 g.

Worked example

(a) Write down the weight that is shown on the scale.

There are two divisions between 70 and 80, so each division represents 5 kg.

75 kg

(b) Write down the number marked with the arrow.

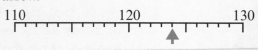

124

There are 10 divisions between 120 and 130 so each division represents 1.

Estimating a scale reading

Sometimes you have to estimate the reading on a scale.

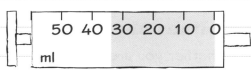

The water doesn't come up to an exact mark but you can make an estimate.

The water is closer to 30 ml than 40 ml.

34 ml is a good estimate.

Now try this

1 Find the number 37 on the number line. Mark it with an arrow (↑).

2 How much water is in this syringe?

150 ml

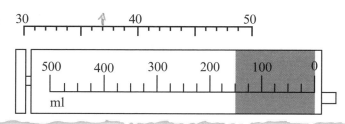

Temperature

You will usually see temperature measured in degrees Celsius (°C) but you may also see it in degrees Fahrenheit (°F).

You need to be able to read temperature scales and work out the difference between two temperatures.

Thermometers

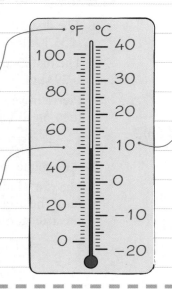

This thermometer shows the temperature in degrees Celsius and degrees Fahrenheit.

The scale on the right shows the temperature in degrees Celsius. The temperature reading is 10°C.

The scale on the left shows the temperature in degrees Fahrenheit. The temperature reading is 50°F.

Water temperatures
Water freezes at 0°C and boils at 100°C

Worked example

This thermometer shows the temperature of a room at different times of the day.

Work out what each mark on the thermometer scale represents. On the scale five marks represent 10°C, so one mark is 10 ÷ 5 = 2°C

Write down the temperatures marked A, B and C.

A 10°C

B 16°C

C 2°C

Now try this

James reads the temperature in his room on three days. What are the temperatures of his room on the three days?

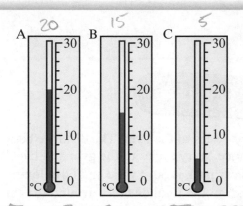

Distances

Distance is a measure of the gap between two points.

The distance between two points is given in units of length.

Distance units

Long distances such as the distance between towns can be measured in kilometres (km) or miles.

The distance between the Earth and the Moon is 384 400 kilometres (km).

The distance between Manchester and London is 262 kilometres (km).

Small distances can be measured in metres (m), centimetres (cm) or millimetres (mm). Small distances can also be measured in feet or inches.

The distance between the top and the bottom of an egg is about 2 inches.

Look at page 34 for a reminder about length.

Worked example

1   The distance between Dover and Calais is 33.1 kilometres (km).

The distance between Calais and Paris is 293 km.

Pierre travels from Dover to Calais, and then on to Paris. How far does he travel?

33.1 + 293 = 326.1 km

2   An athlete ran a total distance of 18 km.

She ran 7 km in the morning and then rested until the afternoon. How far did she run in the afternoon?

18 − 7 = 11 km

If the total distance is 18 km, you can work out the second distance by subtracting the first distance from 18

Worked example

3   Joe drives to work and back each day.
The distance from his home to work is 5.2 miles.

Work out the total distance Joe drives each day.

5.2 + 5.2 = 10.4 miles

Remember to include the units in your answer.

Worked example

4   The diagram shows a school field.
What is the total distance around the field?

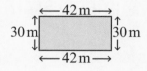

30m + 42m + 30m + 42m = 144m

Write down the whole calculation. Make sure you don't forget any sides by ticking each one off as you go.

Now try this

1   Mary cycles to the gym. The distance between her house and the gym is 3.2 miles. What is the total distance Mary cycles to the gym and back?

2   This car park is 50m wide and 60m long.
Work out the total distance around the car park.

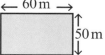

100
120
220m

Routes

You will sometimes see maps with distances labelled that are not to scale. These are useful for working out routes.

Worked example

The diagram shows the distances between attractions at a zoo.

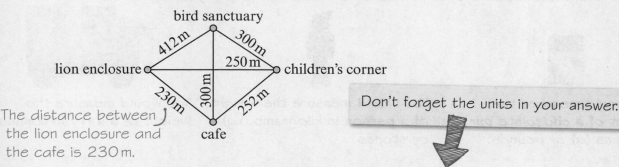

The distance between the lion enclosure and the cafe is 230 m.

(a) What is the distance between the bird sanctuary and the cafe?   300 m

(b) Which attraction is 252 m from the cafe?   children's corner

(c) The Smith family travel from the cafe to children's corner and then to the lion enclosure. Work out the total distance they have travelled.   252 + 250 = 502 m

(d) The Lee family are at the cafe. They want to visit the bird sanctuary and the lion enclosure. They want to walk the shortest route. Plan the shortest route.

Route 1: cafe ⟶ bird sanctuary, bird sanctuary ⟶ lion enclosure
300 + 412 = 712 m
Route 2: cafe ⟶ lion enclosure, lion enclosure ⟶ bird sanctuary
230 + 412 = 642 m
Route 2 is the shortest route.

> Don't forget the units in your answer.

> To find the shortest distance to travel, work out the distance for each possible route.

Now try this

The diagram shows the places that Lily visits each day.
(a) What is the distance between Lily's office and the cafe?   1.5 km
(b) Lily travels from her home to the office. What distance does she travel?   5 km
(c) On one day, Lily travels from her home to a customer before going to the office. What distance does she travel?   8.5 km

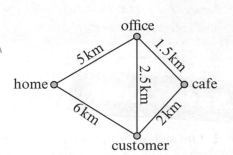

Weight

Weight is a measure of how heavy something is.

Metric units of weight include grams, kilograms and tonnes.

Imperial units of weight include pounds and stones.

Choosing units of weight

Grams or pounds are used to measure light objects.

Kilograms and tonnes or stones are used to measure heavy objects.

You would measure the weight of a chocolate bar in grams (g) or pounds.

You would measure the weight of a person in kilograms (kg) or stones.

You would measure the weight of a lorry in tonnes.

Worked example

(a) Which metric units would you use to measure the weight of a bag of apples?

Grams or kilograms

(b) Mary needs at least 400 g of apples to make a pie. She weighs the apples that she has on the scales below.

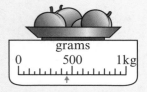

Does Mary have enough apples?

Mary has 450g of apples so she has enough.

> Read the scale carefully and include units in your answer.

Size and weight

Larger objects don't always weigh more and objects of the same size could have different weights.

This box contains pound coins.   This box contains feathers.

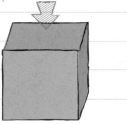   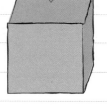

These two boxes are the same size but the box containing coins will be heavier.

Now try this

1 Order these weights from smallest to largest.
   12 tonnes, 12 grams, 12 kilograms   grams, kilograms, tonnes

2 Read the weight on these scales. Remember to include the units in your answer.

| 0 | 100 | 200 | 300 ↓ | 400 | 500 |

grams

350g

Weight calculations

You need to be able to solve problems involving weight.

Kilograms and grams

When comparing or calculating weights, make sure the units are the same.

1 kg = 1000 g

To change kilograms into grams, multiply by 1000.

> Look at page 40 for more about other units of weight.

Using scales

This set of kitchen scales can be used to measure weights in kilograms and grams.

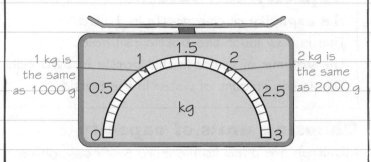

1 kg is the same as 1000 g   2 kg is the same as 2000 g

Worked example

The image shows the weights of four items in a grocery shop.

300 g   200 g   2 kg   400 g

(a) How much do the box of biscuits and the box of chocolates weigh altogether?

300 + 200 = 500 grams

(b) Which is the heaviest item?

2 kg = 2 × 1000 g = 2000 g
The bag of potatoes is heaviest.

(c) What is the total weight of all the items?

300 + 200 + 2000 + 400 = 2900 grams

> Convert the weight in kilograms to grams before comparing the weights.
>
> 1 kg = 1000 g
> so 2 kg = 2 × 1000 g
>   = 2000 g

Now try this

1   How many grams are in 3 kg?   3000g
2   Order these weights from lightest to heaviest.
    8 kg, 800 g, 800 kg, 8 g   8g, 800g, 8kg, 800kg
3   Joe weighed 65 kg. He lost 3 kg. How much does he weigh now? 62kg
4   Mara buys 3 kg of potatoes. She uses 1000 g of potatoes. What weight of potatoes does she have left?

2Kg
2000g

Capacity

Capacity is a measure of how much something can hold.

Some metric units of capacity are litres and millilitres.

Pints are an imperial unit of capacity.

Capacity and volume

The **capacity** of this bottle is 1 litre.
This is how much the bottle can hold.
The **volume** of water in this bottle is 500 millilitres.
This is the amount of water in the bottle.

Choosing units of capacity

Millilitres are used to measure small capacities.

Litres or pints are used to measure larger capacities.

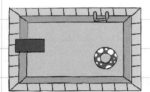

You would measure the capacity of a swimming pool in litres (l).

You would measure the capacity of a milk bottle in litres or pints.

You would measure the capacity of a mug in millilitres (ml).

Worked example

1 (a) Which is larger, 4 litres or 4 millilitres?

4 litres

(b) Would you measure the capacity of a car's petrol tank in litres or millilitres?

litres

(c) Would you measure the capacity of a test tube in litres or millilitres?

millilitres

> Imagine how big an object is to help you decide which units to use to measure it.

Worked example

2 John makes a milkshake. He needs at least 200 ml of milk.

He measures the milk in a measuring jug.

Has John measured enough milk?

No – John has only measured 150 ml.

> Read the scale carefully, then write a statement that answers the question asked.

Look at page 36 for a reminder on how to read scales.

Now try this

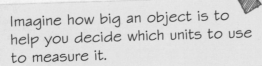

(a) What is the capacity of this measuring jug? 500 ml

(b) What is the volume of liquid in the measuring jug? 300 ml

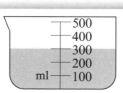

Capacity calculations

You need to be able to solve problems involving capacity.

Litres and millilitres

When solving problems involving capacity you must make sure the units are the same.

1 litre = 1000 ml

To convert litres to millilitres, multiply by 1000.

4000 millilitres (ml) = 4000 ÷ 1000
= 4 litres (l)

Worked example

1 Here are the capacities of three containers.
4000 ml, 3 l, 2.5 l
Work out the total capacity.

4000 ml = 4 litres
Total capacity = 4 + 3 + 2.5 = 9.5 litres

Worked example

2 Jodie had a 2-litre bottle of milk.
She used 250 ml.
How much milk did she have left?

2 litres = 2 × 1000 = 2000 ml
2000 ml − 250 ml = 1750 ml

Problem solved!

✓ Convert all the quantities to the same unit.

✓ Jodie has used some of the milk, so there will be less remaining in the bottle. This means you need to subtract.

Now try this

1 (a) How many millilitres are in 8 litres? 8000 ml

   (b) How many litres are in 2000 ml? 2 L

2 A measuring jug has a capacity of 1.5 litres. Will it be large enough to hold 1800 ml of liquid? no

3 Michael wants to buy the watering can that has the largest capacity.
Which of these cans should he buy?

	Capacity
can A	4500 ml
can B	5500 ml ✓
can C	5 litres

4 Amina is making milkshakes for her 6 friends. She needs 200 ml of milk to make each milkshake.
Should she buy a 1-litre or a 2-litre carton of milk? 200 × 6 = 1200

First work out how much milk Amina needs in total. Then decide whether this is more than 1 litre.

Money

You will use money in everyday life.

Sometimes the money will be in pounds and sometimes in pence.

Often you will deal with money in both pounds and pence.

Converting pounds and pence

100 pence = 1 pound

The digit before the decimal point shows the number of pounds.

£7.50

The two digits after the decimal point show the number of pence.

This means 7 pounds and 50 pence.

Always write money with two digits after the decimal point. This makes it easy to see the difference between £7.50 and £7.05

To convert pounds (£) to pence (p) multiply by 100

× 100

1 pound = 100 pence

÷ 100

To convert pence (p) to pounds (£) divide by 100

Worked example

1 **(a)** Write 4 pounds and 30 pence in figures.

£4.30

(b) Write 5 pounds and 6 pence in figures.

£5.06

30 after the decimal point means 30p.

06 after the decimal point means 6p.

If you work out 120p ÷ 100 on your calculator, you get the answer 1.2

Remember to insert another 0 so that there are two digits after the decimal point.

Worked example

2 **(a)** Convert £3.45 to pence.

£3.45 × 100 = 345p

(b) Convert 28p to pounds.

28p ÷ 100 = £0.28

(c) Convert 120p to pounds.

120p ÷ 100 = £1.20

Now try this

1 Write: **(a)** 245p in pounds (£) _£2.45_ **(b)** £4.56 in pence (p) _456p_ **(c)** 350p in pounds (£). _£3.50_

2 Write 6 pounds and 20 pence in pounds (£). _£6.20_

3 Kanata spent 6 pounds and 5 pence on his shopping.

Circle the two amounts in the list that are equal to 6 pounds and 5 pence.

£6.5   (605p)   650p   (£6.05)   £6.50

Money calculations

You need to be able to solve problems involving money.

Worked example

1 Joshua buys some stationery.

A notepad costs £3.99 and a pen costs 65p.

Joshua pays with a £5 note. How much change does he get?

65p ÷ 100 = £0.65
£3.99 + £0.65 = £4.64
£5.00 − £4.64 = £0.36

Problem solved!

✓ You need to make the units the same – either all in pounds or all in pence.

✓ Change the price of the pen from pence to pounds by dividing by 100.

✓ Both prices are now in the same units so add them together.

✓ Subtract the cost from £5.00 to find out how much change Joshua gets.

Worked example

2 In one shop a laptop costs £349. In another shop the same laptop costs £299.

What is the difference in price between the two shops?

£349 × £299 = £50

The prices of the laptops are both in pounds so you don't need to convert to the same unit.

To work out the difference you need to subtract.

Worked example

3 At the supermarket, 1 can of drink costs 70p. If you buy 5 cans you can save £1.00

At the corner shop, 1 can costs 60p.

Which is the cheapest place to buy 5 cans?

Supermarket:
5 × 70 = 350p = £3.50
Save £1: £3.50 − £1 = £2.50

Corner shop:
5 × 60 = 300p = £3.00
The supermarket is cheaper.

Work out the cost of 5 cans with each offer.

Make sure your answers are in the same units to compare them.

Now try this

4·30

1 Gemma and her child travel by bus. The cost of an adult ticket is £3.40 and the cost of a child ticket is 90p. How much does it cost them to travel by bus?

2 Zara and 4 friends want to have afternoon tea. Which cafe is cheapest for them?

Cafe 1

Afternoon tea
£6.75 per person
Save £1.25 per person for groups of more than 4 people.

27.50 cafe 1

Afternoon Tea
£6.75 per person or £28 for 5 people.

cafe 2

45

Problem-solving practice

When you are solving problems, you need to:

- ✓ read the question
- ✓ check your answers
- ✓ decide which calculation you are going to use
- ✓ make sure you have answered the question asked.

---

1 Jodie measures the height of a plant. It measures 80 mm. She expects it to grow by 7 mm each week.

How tall does she expect the plant to be in 10 weeks?

$10 \times 7 = 70$

$80 + 70 = 150 \text{ mm}$

Length page 34

Work out how much Jodie expects the plant to grow in 10 weeks. Then add this amount to 80 mm.

TOP TIP

Remember to write units with your answer.

---

2 Marcus is making a cake. He needs 300 g of flour.

The scales show how much flour he has.

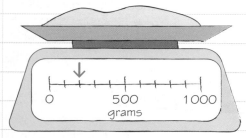

How much more flour does he need to make the cake?   100 g

Reading scales page 36, Weight page 40

Read the scales to find out how much flour Marcus has.

Compare the reading with how much flour he needs.

TOP TIP

Use subtraction to find out how much more flour Marcus needs.

---

3 A cup can hold 200 ml of liquid.

Abraham needs to make 12 cups of tea for his colleagues. He has enough hot water in a flask to make 2 litres of tea. Does he have enough water?   NO

You must show all your working.

$12 \times 200 = 2400$

$2 \text{ litres} = 2000 \text{ ml}$

Capacity page 42

Change 2 litres to millilitres.

TOP TIP

Start by converting so that both of the amounts are in the same units. Then think carefully about what calculations you need to carry out.

Problem-solving practice

4 On the scale there is a large block of cheese and a small block of cheese.

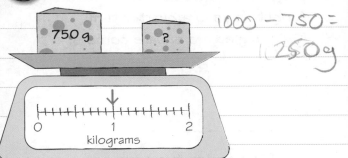

750 g   ?

kilograms

$1000 - 750 =$
$1.250 g$

Work out the weight of the small block of cheese.

Reading scales page 36

Read the scales to find out the total weight of both blocks of cheese.

Work out how much more you need to add to 750 g to get to the total weight.

TOP TIP

Remember that both quantities need to be in the same units.

Convert the reading on the scale to grams.

---

5 The map shows the distance between Abby's house and her three friends' houses.

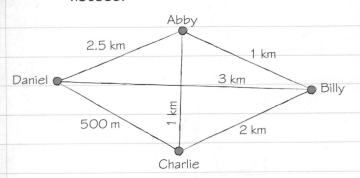

Abby
2.5 km   1 km
3 km
Daniel   Billy
1 km
500 m   2 km
Charlie

(a) What is the distance between Abby's house and Daniel's house? 2·5km

(b) Abby visited Charlie and then Billy and then returned home. 4km
What is the total distance she travelled?

Distances page 38, Routes page 39

(b) Put your finger on Abby's house and trace the journeys. Add up the total distances.

TOP TIP

Be systematic.

Write down the distance between Abby's house and Charlie's house, and then the distance between Charlie's house and Billy's house.

Remember Abby travels back home from Billy's house.

---

6 A chocolate bar costs £1.50 and a can of drink costs 85p.

(a) Alonso has a £10 note and wants to buy 5 chocolate bars and 2 cans of drink. Does he have enough money? Yes

(b) How much change will he get? £1

5
$5 \times 1·50 = 7·50$
$2 \times ·85 = 1·70$
£9

Money calculations page 45

Convert the total cost of the cans to pounds by dividing by 100.

TOP TIP

Work out the cost of 5 chocolate bars and 2 cans of drink. Then subtract the total from £10 to see if he has enough money.

Angles

Angles are a measure of turn.

Large and small angles

An angle is a point where two straight lines meet.

Examples of angles are the corners of shapes.

This is an angle.

Small angles look 'sharp'. Large angles look 'blunt' or 'flat'.

This is the largest angle.

This is the smallest angle.

Right angles

A right angle is a quarter turn.

Right angles are square corners.

This is a right angle.

All of the angles in a square or a rectangle are right angles.

Measuring angles

Angles are measured in degrees (°).

A right angle is 90°.

Worked example

Write down the number of right angles in each of these shapes.

(a)

four right angles

(b)

no right angles

(c)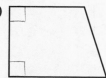

two right angles

A square always has four right angles.

Each of these angles is larger than a right angle.

Now try this

1 Write down the number of right angles in each of these shapes.

(a) 0

(b)

(c) 4

2 Write down the letter of the largest angle in each of these shapes.

(a)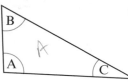

(b)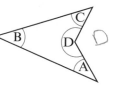

Symmetry

Some shapes have lines of symmetry.

Lines of symmetry

A line of symmetry is a mirror line. One half of the shape is a mirror image of another.

These shapes have one line of symmetry.

If you fold the shape on the mirror line, the sides will fit together exactly.

Using tracing paper

You are allowed to ask for tracing paper in your exam. You can use it to check for lines of symmetry.

Worked example

1 Draw the lines of symmetry on these shapes.

(a)

one line of symmetry

(b)

no lines of symmetry

(c)

four lines of symmetry

Draw the mirror line as a dotted line.

Some shapes have no lines of symmetry.

Some shapes have more than one line of symmetry. Make sure you look for all of them.

Now try this

Shape (c) has more than one line of symmetry.

Copy the shapes and draw the lines of symmetry.

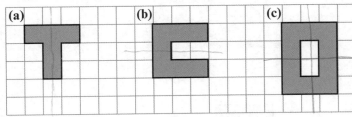

(a)   (b)   (c)

2D shapes

Two-dimensional (2D) shapes are flat.

2D shapes

These are all 2D shapes.

A polygon is a 2D shape where all the sides are straight lines.

Triangles

Triangles are 2D shapes with three straight sides and three angles.

Circles

A circle is a 2D shape with one curved side.

Quadrilaterals

Quadrilaterals are 2D shapes with four straight sides and four angles.

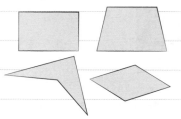

Squares and rectangles are special kinds of quadrilaterals – each has four right angles.

Squares and rectangles

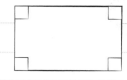

Rectangles have four right angles. Opposite sides are the same length.

Squares have four right angles and all the sides are the same length.

Worked example

Sasha is choosing a template for a new company logo. She decides to make the background square. Which template should she use?

Template B

The square has equal sides and four right angles.

For a reminder about right angles look at page 48.

Now try this

Write the names of these shapes.

(a)
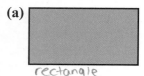
rectangle

(b)

triangle

(c)
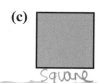
square

3D shapes

A three-dimensional (3D) shape is solid.

Faces, edges and corners

This 3D shape has 6 faces, 12 edges and 8 corners.

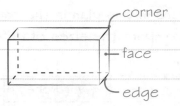

corner

face

edge

3D shapes

Here are some 3D shapes.

A cube has six square faces.

The faces of a cuboid are rectangles.

Four of the faces of this pyramid are triangles.

cube

cuboid

pyramid

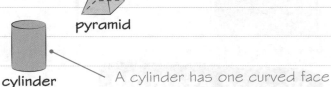

sphere

cone

cylinder

A cylinder has one curved face and two flat circular faces.

A sphere has one curved face and no corners.

A cone has one curved face and one flat circular face.

3D shapes in everyday life

You will see 3D shapes in everyday life.

This tin of paint is a cylinder.

This box of chocolates is a cuboid.

You need to count all the faces including the hidden faces.

Worked example

Liang buys this box of chocolates.

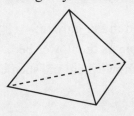

(a) What shape is the box?

pyramid

(b) Write down the number of faces on the shape.

4 faces

Now try this

1 Name these 3D shapes.

(a)   **(b)**   **(c)**

cube   cuboid   cylinder

2 How many corners does this cube have?

     8

Using plans

A plan shows the layout of objects in a space as if you were looking directly down from above.

Each square in this plan is the same size.
You can compare the sizes of different objects by counting the squares.

door

wardrobe

drawers

window

bed

The wardrobe is four squares long.
The chest of drawers is two squares long.

The wardrobe is twice the length of the chest of drawers.

The bed is two squares wide and four squares long. It covers eight squares.

Worked example

This plan shows the layout of objects in Jo's garden.

(a) What shape is the patio?

rectangle

(b) How many squares is the patio?

21 squares

(c) Jo wants to put a shed in her garden.
The shed is twice as big as the flower bed.
Draw a rectangle to show where the shed could go.

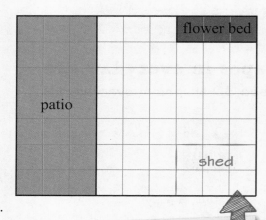

There are different positions where you can put the shed.

Now try this

Here is a plan of Sarah's living room.

(a) What shape are the shelves? Rectangle

(b) How many squares is the sofa? 4

(c) Sarah wants to put a table in her room.
The table is twice as big as the shelves.
The table is square.

Copy the plan and draw a square to show where the dining table could go.

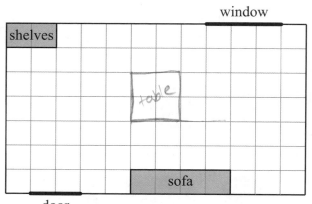

Problem-solving practice

When you are solving problems, you need to:

- ✓ read the question
- ✓ check your answers
- ✓ decide which calculation you are going to use
- ✓ make sure you have answered the question asked.

---

1 Which of these shapes has exactly two lines of symmetry?

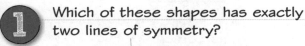
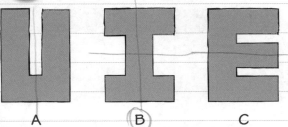

A   B   C

Symmetry page 49

Draw the lines of symmetry on each shape.

TOP TIP

Remember to look for all the lines of symmetry.

---

2 Shade one more square in this diagram so that the diagram has exactly one line of symmetry.

Symmetry page 49

Sketch the square in different positions and check the lines of symmetry.

TOP TIP

Make sure the diagram has no more than one line of symmetry.

---

3 (a) Circle the shapes that are quadrilaterals.

(b) Write numbers to complete this sentence.

A rectangle has ....4........ right angles and ....2.......... lines of symmetry.

2D shapes page 50, Symmetry page 49

Count the number of sides each shape has to decide which shapes are quadrilaterals.

TOP TIP

Sketch a rectangle to help you answer part (b). Count the number of right angles and draw in the lines of symmetry.

Problem-solving practice

 Robert is choosing a gift. He sees chocolate boxes that come in these three shapes.

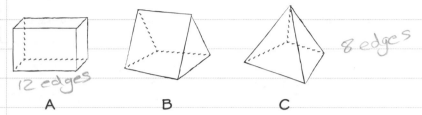

12 edges

8 edges

A   B   C

(a) Which of the boxes has 5 faces, 9 edges and 6 corners?   B

(b) Write the number of edges of the other two boxes.

3D shapes page 51

Count the number of faces, sides and corners for each shape.

TOP TIP

Write the number of faces, sides and corners for each shape clearly next to the shape so you can find the correct answer.

 The plan shows Karen's living room.

window

TV

shelves

door

sofa

(a) What shape is the space for the TV?   Triangle

(b) Karen buys some shelves.

The shelves are half the size of the sofa.

Karen wants to put the shelves on a wall of her living room.

Show the shelves on the plan.

Using plans page 52

There are different positions where you can put the shelves and you may need to turn them so that they fit. Try different positions and check that they are on the wall.

TOP TIP

You could draw the shelves on a separate piece of paper and see where they fit on a wall.

Lists

When data is collected it can be displayed in a list. Lists can contain words and numbers.

Listing information

You can organise lists to make them easier to understand.

Here is a list of the prices in a cafe.

Sandwiches	
Cheese salad	£2.00
Tuna salad	£2.50
Egg mayonnaise	£1.90
Drinks	
Coffee	£2.00
Tea	£1.50

Items are listed in sections so that it is easy to find what you want.

Ordered lists

Sometimes information is displayed in a particular order.

This recipe is written as an ordered list of steps.

Pancake recipe
1. Mix the flour, eggs and milk.
2. Heat the frying pan.
3. Fry the pancakes on both sides.
4. Serve with sugar and lemon.

You need to carry out the steps in the order in which they are written.

Worked example

1 Here is a list of the prices in a garage.

   MOT: £45
   Interim service: £115
   Full service: £195
   Oil change: £50

   Cheng has a full service and an MOT.
   How much does it cost him?

   45 + 195 = £240

Find the information you need in the list, then add the numbers together.

Worked example

2 Connor recorded the times it took his friends to complete a puzzle.

   Joe: 45 seconds
   Theo: 30 seconds
   Marie: 32 seconds
   Lina: 43 seconds

   Which person took the shortest time to complete the puzzle?

   Theo, 30 seconds

The shortest time anyone took is the lowest number in the list.

Now try this

The list shows the prices of food in a restaurant.

(a) What is the most expensive main meal? Burger

(b) Find the cost of soup of the day and a burger and fries. £14·45

(c) What is the difference in price between the apple pie and the ice cream? 50p

$$\begin{array}{r} \overset{2}{\cancel{3}}^{1}\!45 - \\ 2.95 \\ \hline 0.50 \end{array}$$

$$\begin{array}{r} 4.95 \\ 9.50 \\ \hline 14.45 \end{array}$$

Starters	
Soup of the day	£4.95
Prawn cocktail	£5.20
Main meal	
Fish pie	£8.99
Burger and fries	£9.50
Vegetarian quiche	£7.95
Desserts	
Apple pie	£3.45
Ice cream	£2.95

Tables

You need to be able to find information in tables so that you can solve problems.

This table shows information about car stopping distances at different speeds.

Speed	Stopping distance
20 miles per hour	12 metres
30 miles per hour	23 metres
40 miles per hour	36 metres

Find out the stopping distance of a car by finding its speed in the table and reading along the row.
At 30 miles per hour the stopping distance is 23 metres.

Worked example

1 This table shows the costs of hotel rooms for one night during peak season.

Room	Cost
single	£85
standard double	£105
standard twin	£110
deluxe double	£180
deluxe twin	£200

(a) How much will it cost to book a standard double room for one night during peak season?

£105

(b) What is the difference in cost between a deluxe twin room and a standard twin room for one night?

£200 − £110 = £90

Look for the cost of a deluxe twin for one night, then look for the cost of a standard twin. Find the difference by subtracting.

Worked example

2 Joshua did a survey to find out how people listened to music.

The table shows the results.

	Online	CD
Men	12	7
Women	15	10

How many men listened to music with a CD?

7

Put one finger on the men row and read across. Put another finger on the CD column and read down. Where your fingers meet is the number of men that listened to music with a CD.

Now try this

This table shows information about two second hand cars that are for sale.

(a) What is the cost of car A? 5,000

(b) What is the engine size of car B? 1.6cc

(c) Work out the difference in mileage between the two cars.
12 000

	Car A	Car B
Engine size	1.3 cc	1.6 cc
Mileage	42 000	30 000
Cost	£5,000	£7,000

Tally charts

A tally chart is a table that is used to record information collected in an experiment or survey. You can use the totals of the tally to record the frequency with which something happens.

This tally chart shows the number of drinks sold in a cafe one morning.

Drink	Tally	Frequency
tea	III	3
coffee	HHI II	7
fruit juice	HHI HHI IIII	14
water	HHI	5

A tally is useful for collecting information. For each drink sold, draw a line.

The frequency tells you the number of drinks sold.

You can work out the frequency from the tally. There are 3 lines in the tally column for tea so the number of teas sold is 3

To show the number 5, draw four tally lines with a line through them.

Worked example

Dinah is organising a meal for her friends and needs to order desserts before they arrive.

Here are the orders.

ice cream, apple pie, trifle, ice cream, ice cream, apple pie, trifle, trifle, trifle, apple pie, ice cream, ice cream, ice cream, apple pie, trifle, trifle, trifle, apple pie, trifle, trifle

(a) Complete this tally chart to show how many of each dessert was ordered.

Dessert	Tally	Frequency
ice cream	HHI I	6
apple pie	HHI	5
trifle	HHI IIII	9

(b) Which dessert is most popular?

Trifle

Problem solved!

✓ Use a system to make sure you don't miss any of the orders.

✓ Cross off each order when you have written the tally. This will help you not to miss any pieces of data.

✓ Check that you have included all the data. $6 + 5 + 9 = 20$
There are 20 orders so this is correct.

✓ To find the most popular dessert, look at the 'Frequency' column and find the highest number.

Now try this

A museum shop recorded the items bought during one day.

(a) Complete the tally and frequency table.

Item	Tally	Frequency
postcard	HHI HHI HHI HHI II	22
key ring	HHI HHI	10
book	HHI HHI III	13
poster	HHI III	8

(b) How many items were bought from the shop that day? 53

Reading bar charts

You can use a bar chart to represent data from a tally chart or frequency table. This bar chart shows the number of houses sold by an estate agent each month.

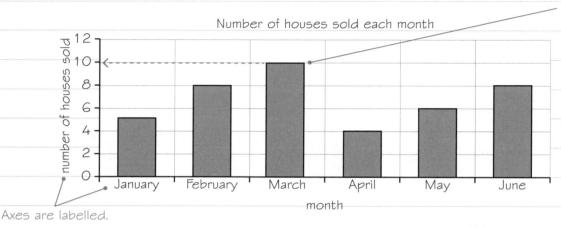

Number of houses sold each month

The height of the bar shows you the frequency – the number of houses that were sold.

Axes are labelled.

Worked example

The bar chart shows the number of tablets sold by Mark in one week.

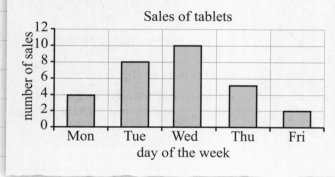

Sales of tablets

(a) How many tablets did Mark sell on Thursday?

5

(b) On which day did Mark sell the fewest tablets?

Friday

(c) How many tablets did Mark sell during the week?

4 + 8 + 10 + 5 + 2 = 29

✓ Write down the number of tablets sold on Monday, Tuesday, Wednesday, Thursday and Friday.

✓ Add up the values to find the number of tablets Mark sold during the week.

Now try this

The bar chart shows the number of scarves of different colours sold at a market stall on Saturday.

(a) How many blue scarves were sold? 6

(b) Which colour was sold the most? cream

(c) How many scarves were sold altogether?

8 + 6 + 12 + 7 = 33

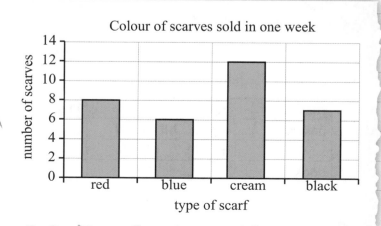

Colour of scarves sold in one week

Work out how many of each colour of scarf was sold first.

Completing a bar chart

You need to know how to complete bar charts.

Adding a bar to a bar chart

To add a bar to a bar chart:

✓ Read the labels on the horizontal axis to find where your bar needs to go.

✓ Read the values on the vertical axis to find how tall your bar needs to be.

✓ Use a pencil and ruler to draw your bar.

Bar chart features

- ✓ Bars are the same width.
- ✓ There are equal gaps between the bars.
- ✓ The chart has a title.
- ✓ Both axes have labels.
- ✓ The height (or length) of each bar represents the frequency.

Worked example

For a reminder about reading bar charts look at page 58.

The bar chart shows the number of milkshakes sold by a cafe in one week.

Number of milkshakes sold in one week

vertical axis: number of milkshakes (0 to 10)
horizontal axis: day of the week — Mon, Tue, Wed, Thu, Fri

- ✓ Find Friday on the horizontal axis.
- ✓ Find 4 on the vertical axis.
- ✓ Use a ruler to draw your bar.
- ✓ Make your bar the same width as the other bars.

The number of milkshakes sold on Friday was 4.

Draw a bar for Friday to complete the chart.

Now try this

The chart shows the number of bookings at a caravan site over a period of five months. There were 10 bookings in June. Complete the bar chart.

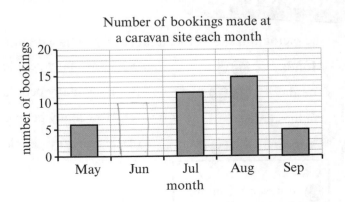

Number of bookings made at a caravan site each month

vertical axis: number of bookings (0 to 20)
horizontal axis: month — May, Jun, Jul, Aug, Sep

Reading pictograms

You can use a pictogram to represent data from a tally chart or frequency table.

This pictogram shows the results of a survey about how people watch television. There is one row for each option.

A pictogram must have a key. This tells you how many items are represented by each picture.

Key: 📺 represents 2 people

terrestrial	📺📺📺📺📺📺
satellite	📺📺📺📺📺
cable	📺
internet	📺📺📺📺

📺 represents 2 people so 12 people said they watched television using terrestrial.

Each television represents 2 people, so half a television represents 1 person. This row represents 9 people.

To work out the total number of people in the survey, add together the totals of each row:
12 + 9 + 2 + 7 = 30

Worked example

The pictogram shows the numbers of board games Bettina played in June, July and August.

June	▦▦▍
July	▦▦
August	▦▪

Key: ▦ represents 4 board games

How many board games did Bettina play in August?

5

Use the key to work out what each picture represents.

▦ = 4 games　▌= 3 games

▊ = 2 games　▪ = 1 game

There is a block of 4 squares and a block of 1 square in August. This represents 4 + 1 = 5 board games.

Now try this

The pictogram shows the number of people who hired a rowing boat over four days.

Monday　●◖
Tuesday　●●
Wednesday　◖
Thursday　●●◖

Key:
● represents 2 people

(a) How many people hired the boat on Tuesday? 4

(b) How many people hired the boat on Wednesday? 1

(c) How many people hired the boat on Thursday? 5

(d) How many people in total hired the boat over the four days? 13

Reading pie charts

A pie chart is a circle divided into slices called sectors.

In a pie chart, the whole circle represents a set of data.

Each sector represents a fraction of the data.

This pie chart represents the matches won, lost and drawn by a football team.

Results of football matches

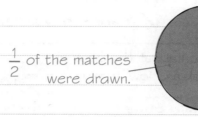

$\frac{1}{2}$ of the matches were drawn.

$\frac{1}{4}$ of the matches were lost.

■ wins ☐ losses ■ draws

Worked example

The pie chart shows information about items of clothing sold in a shop last month.

Clothes sold last month

■ T-shirts ■ trousers ■ skirts

(a) Which item did the shop sell the most of?

T-shirts

Look at the largest sector in the pie chart.

(b) What fraction of the items sold were trousers?

$\frac{1}{4}$

Look at the sector that represents trousers. What fraction of the pie chart is this?

See page 15 for more about fractions.

(c) The shop sold 60 T-shirts. How many items did they sell in total?

$2 \times 60 = 120$

$\frac{1}{2}$ of the pie chart shows T-shirts.

If $\frac{1}{2}$ is 60 items, the whole is $2 \times 60 = 120$

Now try this

The pie chart shows the orders made at a takeaway in one week.

Customers chose either a pizza, noodles or fish and chips.

(a) Which meal was the most popular? Pizza

(b) What fraction of the orders were noodles? $\frac{1}{4}$

(c) The takeaway had 80 customers that week.
How many people ordered pizza? 40

Orders in one week

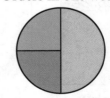

☐ pizza ■ noodles ■ fish and chips

Had a go ☐ Nearly there ☐ Nailed it! ☐

Problem-solving practice

When you are solving problems, you need to:
- ✓ read the question
- ✓ decide which calculation you are going to use
- ✓ check your answers
- ✓ make sure you have answered the question asked.

1 The table shows information about the cost of a holiday apartment in peak and low season.

	Adult price	Child price
Low season	£120	£80
Peak season	£170	£95

The Smiths are a family of two adults and two children.

(a) How much would it cost the Smith family to stay in the holiday apartment during low season? 240 + 160 = £400

(b) How much would it cost the Smith family to stay in the holiday apartment during peak season? 340 + 190 = 530

(c) What is the difference in price? 130

Tables page 56

(a) Look across the row for low season. The cost for the Smith family will be 2 × .... + 2 × ....

(b) Repeat part (a) but this time look at the row for peak season.

(c) Subtract your answer to part (a) from your answer to part (b)

TOP TIP

Set out your work clearly. You can use a calculator but don't forget to check each line of your working.

2 Paul is taking a drinks order for his colleagues at work.

The tally chart shows what they ask for.

Drink	Tally	Frequency
coffee	𝍸	5
tea	𝍸 II	7
hot chocolate	IIII	4

(a) Complete the frequency column in the table.

(b) Which was the most popular order? Tea

(c) How many people did Paul ask? 16

Tally charts page 57

Remember 𝍸 means 5 orders.

Add up all the frequencies to find out how many people Paul asked in total.

TOP TIP

Be careful when writing the frequency. Make sure you write it in the correct cell in the table.

3 This list gives an athlete's best training times for the 110 m hurdles.

Time (seconds)
12.8
13.8
12.4

What is the difference between his fastest and slowest times?

13·8 −
12·4
01·4

Lists page 55

Look for the fastest time and slowest time in the list.

Subtract the fastest time from the slowest time to find the difference.

TOP TIP

Remember to give the units in your answer.

Problem-solving practice

4 The bar chart shows the number of ice creams sold by a shop in one week.

Ice cream sales in one week

(a) How many ice creams were sold on Thursday? 6

(b) Which day had the fewest ice cream sales? Friday

(c) How many ice creams were sold altogether? 33

Reading bar charts page 58

Look at the scale on the bar chart.

For part (c), write the total number of ice creams sold each day and then add them up.

TOP TIP

Write a list of the days and the numbers of ice creams sold. Check you have added five numbers, one for each day.

5 The table shows information about the number of calls a sales person made each day in a week.

Day	Mon	Tue	Wed	Thu	Fri
Number of calls	4	6	2	5	?

The sales person made 20 calls during the week.

(a) How many calls did he make on Friday? 3

(b) Complete this bar chart to represent the number of calls he made.

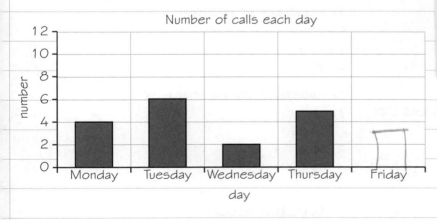

Number of calls each day

Completing a bar chart page 59

Make sure you understand the scale.

The bars must be the same width and the gaps must be of equal size.

TOP TIP

Halfway between 2 and 4 is 3. Label 1, 3, 5, 7, 9 on the vertical axis.

Answers

NUMBER

1 Whole numbers
1) two
2) (a) five hundred and twenty-one
   (b) six hundred and two
   (c) 402
   (d) 520
3) (a) 4 hundreds   (b) 4 tens   (c) 4 units

2 Comparing numbers
1) 320
2) (a) 942
   (b) 249
3) 203, 230, 234, 243

3 Adding
1) £443
2) 441

4 Subtracting
1) 5 hours
2) £37
3) No she doesn't have enough.
   $10 - 4 = 6$
   She has £6 left which is less than £8
4) £181

5 Multiplication
1) 184
2) 260 people
3) Yes, twelve cartons cost £24
4) £140
5) £68

6 Division
1) 25
2) £18
3) 36

7 Multiplying and dividing by 10, 100 and 1000
1) (a) 120   (b) 300   (c) 52
2) (a) 1000   (b) 120   (c) 10

8 Remainders
1) (a) 15   (b) 6
2) 3

9 Choosing the right order
1) £380
2) £2
3) £50

10 Using a calculator
1) £208
2) 28 tables

11 Multiples
1) (a) 3, 6, 9, 12, 15
   (b) 4, 8, 12, 16, 20
2) 3, 5, 7, 9, 11
3) No, because £1 + 50p + 50p = £2.00 exactly

12 Number patterns
11

13 Decimals
1) (a) 6 and 7   (b) 0 and 1
2) (a) 3 tenths   (b) 3 hundredths
3) one

14 Ordering decimals
1) (a) 6.72   (b) 23.8
2) £20.30, £22.03, £22.30, £23.02

15 Fractions
1) $\frac{1}{5}$
2) (a) one-quarter   (b) one-third   (c) one-tenth

16 Types of fractions
1) (a) $\frac{2}{5}$
   (b) $\frac{1}{5}$
   (c) $\frac{2}{5}$
2) four-fifths

17 Equivalent fractions
1) (a) yes   (b) no   (c) yes
2) $\frac{2}{6}$
3) $\frac{7}{7}$

18 Fractions of amounts
(a) £30
(b) £15
(c) 12 g

19 Rounding whole numbers
1) (a) 70
   (b) 320
2) (a) 400
   (b) 600
3) £800

20 Rounding money
1) (a) £7   (b) £8   (c) £257   (d) £421
2) £4
3) £2
4) £436
5) No she is not correct. £5.36 is £5 to the nearest pound.

21 Estimating

1) (a) 60 + 70 = 130

   (b) 900 − 300 = 600

   (c) 50 × 10 = 500

2) £3 + £5 = £8

22 Checking your answer

1) 80 + 100 − 90 = 90
   His answer is not close to 90 so he is incorrect.

2) (a) correct

   (b) incorrect

   (c) incorrect

   (d) correct

23 Problem-solving practice

1) £3

2) (a) £6,000

   (b) £486

3) (a) 18 packets

   (b) 8 screws are left over

24 Problem-solving practice

4) 134

5) (a)

week 1	week 2	week 3	week 4	week 5
10	14	18	22	26

   (b) 30

6) £2 + £9 + £4 + £1 + £2 = £18

7) 12.04 seconds
   12.40 seconds
   12.47 seconds

TIME

25 Calendars

(a) Saturday 11 July

(b) Sunday 19 July

(c) Thursday 16 July

26 Units of time

5 hours

27 12-hour clock

(a) 3.30 p.m. or three thirty in the afternoon

(b) 8.00 p.m. or 8 o'clock in the evening

(c) 3.45 p.m. or quarter to four in the afternoon

28 24-hour clock

1) (a) 2.45 p.m.

   (b) 14:45

2)

12-hour	24-hour
3.12 a.m.	03:12
7.50 p.m.	19:50
11.30 p.m.	23:30
2.15 p.m.	14:15

29 Time calculations

1) 14:00

2) 3 hours

3) 11:30

30 Timetables

(a) 06:25

(b) (i) 06:30   **(ii)** 10 minutes

31 Problem-solving practice

1) Yes, the cake will be ready in time.

2) 3 hours and 30 minutes

3) 17:00

32 Problem-solving practice

4) (a) 09:50   **(b)** 10:30   **(c)** 40 minutes

5) (a) 13:30   **(b)** 17:00   **(c)** 3 hours and 30 minutes

MEASURES

33 Units

1) (a) A shop sells 2 <u>pint</u> bottles of milk. The milk is stored in a fridge at 5 <u>degrees Celsius</u>.

   (b) Bob is buying a new kitchen. The width of the kitchen is 4.5 <u>metres</u>. His kitchen table is flat-packed and weighs 25 <u>kilograms</u>.

2) The units are incorrect, centimetres are a measure of length.

34 Length

1) (a) 4 km   **(b)** 1 foot

2) 5.5 feet

3) 2 m

4) 53 mm

35 Measuring lengths

1) (a) 2 cm   **(b)** 3.8 cm

2) Accept between 8 m and 10 m.

36 Reading scales

1)

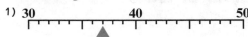

2) 150 ml

37 Temperature

A: 20 °C, B: 15 °C, C: 5 °C

38 Distances

1) 6.4 miles

2) 220 m

39 Routes

(a) 1.5 km   **(b)** 5 km   **(c)** 8.5 km

40 Weight

1) 12 grams, 12 kilograms, 12 tonnes

2) 350 g

Answers

41 Weight calculations
1) 3000 g
2) 8 g, 800 g, 8 kg, 800 kg
3) 62 kg
4) 2 kg or 2000 g

42 Capacity
(a) 500 ml   (b) 300 ml

43 Capacity calculations
1) (a) 8000 ml   (b) 2 litres
2) No, 1.5 litres is 1500 ml which is less than 1800 ml.
3) can B
4) A 2-litre carton of milk. She needs 6 × 200 = 1200 ml of milk. The 1-litre bottle only contains 1000 ml of milk, which is not enough. The 2-litre bottle contains 2000 ml of milk, which is enough.

44 Money
1) (a) £2.45   (b) 456p   (c) £3.50
2) £6.20
3) 605p and £6.05

45 Money calculations
1) £4.30
2) Cafe 1 costs £27.50, cafe 2 costs £28. So cafe 1 is cheaper.

46 Problem-solving practice
1) 150 mm
2) 100 g
3) No. He has enough for 2000 ml but he needs enough for 2400 ml.

47 Problem-solving practice
4) 250 g
5) (a) 2.5 km   (b) 4 km
6) (a) Yes   (b) £0.80 or 80p

SHAPE AND SPACE

48 Angles
1) (a) 0
   (b) 1
   (c) 4
2) (a) A
   (b) D

49 Symmetry

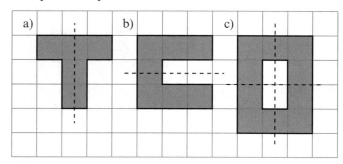

50 2D shapes
(a) rectangle
(b) triangle
(c) square

51 3D shapes
1) (a) cube   (b) cuboid   (c) cylinder
2) 8

52 Using plans
(a) rectangle
(b) 4 squares
(c) The table can be anywhere on the grid but is made up of four squares arranged as shown.

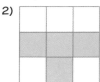

53 Problem-solving practice
1) shape B
2)

3) (a)

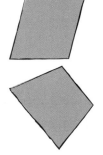

(b) A rectangle has <u>four</u> right-angles and <u>two</u> lines of symmetry.

54 Problem-solving practice
4) (a) shape B
   (b) A: 12 sides, C: 8 sides

5) **(a)** triangle

(b) The shelves can be put in lots of different places. Here is one possible position.

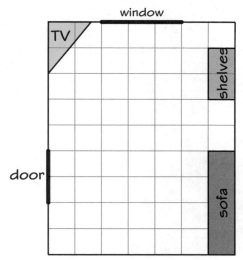

HANDLING DATA

55 Lists

(a) burger and fries

(b) £14.45

(c) £0.50

56 Tables

(a) £5,000   **(b)** 1.6cc   **(c)** 12000 miles

57 Tally charts

(a)

Item	Tally	Frequency
postcards	IIII IIII IIII IIII II	22
key rings	IIII IIII	10
book	IIII IIII III	13
poster	IIII III	8

(b) 53

58 Reading bar charts

(a) 6

(b) cream

(c) 33

59 Completing a bar chart

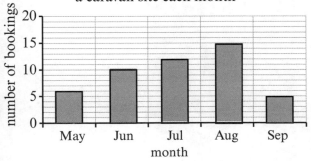

60 Reading pictograms

(a) 4 people

(b) 1 person

(c) 5 people

(d) 13 people

61 Reading pie charts

(a) pizza

(b) $\frac{1}{4}$

(c) 40

62 Problem-solving practice

1) **(a)** £400

(b) £530

(c) £130

2) **(a)**

Drink	Tally	Frequency
coffee	IIII	5
tea	IIII II	7
hot chocolate	IIII	4

(b) tea

(c) 16

3) 1.4 seconds

63 Problem-solving practice

4) **(a)** 6

(b) Friday

(c) 33

5) **(a)** 3

(b)

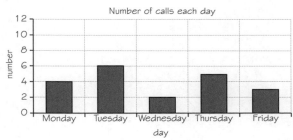

Notes

Notes

Published by Pearson Education Limited, 80 Strand, London, WC2R 0RL.

www.pearsonschoolsandfecolleges.co.uk

Copies of official specifications for all Edexcel qualifications may be found on the website: www.edexcel.com

Text © Pearson Education Limited 2017
Edited, typeset and produced by Elektra Media Ltd
Original illustrations © Pearson Education Limited 2017
Illustrated by Elektra Media Ltd
Cover illustration by Miriam Sturdee

The right of Sharon Bolger to be identified as author of this work has been asserted by her in accordance with the Copyright, Designs and Patents Act 1988.

First published 2017

20 19 18 17
10 9 8 7 6 5 4 3 2 1

British Library Cataloguing in Publication Data
A catalogue record for this book is available from the British Library

ISBN 978 1 292 14568 6

Printed in Slovakia by Neografia